DISCARD

Trout Fly
Patterns

Taff Price

whitecap

This book is dedicated to the memory of Harry 'Tex'
Ranger, my friend and father-in-law, who tied some of
the original flies for this and other books of mine. He
died suddenly during the preparation of this book. He
will be sorely missed.

A Pyramid Paperback

First published in Great Britain in 2005 by
Hamlyn, a division of Octopus Publishing Group Ltd
2–4 Heron Quays, London E14 4JP

Published in the U.S. and Canada by Whitecap Books Ltd

For more information, contact
Whitecap Books, 351 Lynn Avenue, North Vancouver,
British Columbia, Canada V7J 2C4
www.whitecap.ca

This material was previously published as
Fly Patterns: an International Guide

ISBN 1 55285 730 1
EAN 9781552857304

Printed and bound in China

10 9 8 7 6 5 4 3 2 1

contents

introduction

It is now almost 20 years since this book was first published and many developments in the world of fly-fishing and fly-tying have occurred, new flies have been introduced and new fishing techniques have been developed.

Fishing rods, reels, hooks, leader material and fly lines have been improved, adding to the enjoyment and ultimate success of fly-fishing. Fly-tiers are using more man-made materials in their fly-tying; all sorts of shimmering, glistening, and attractive tinsels, chenilles, and artificial winging mediums are employed, and some of the new flies depicted in this edition show this development. Fishing with the artificial fly in saltwater is one of the growth areas in our sport, adding a huge dimension to the gentle art of fly-fishing and fly-tying.

The practice of "catch and release" and the increased use of barbless hooks are indicative of how seriously today's fly fishermen take environmental and species protection. The world is a much smaller place and fly fishermen are seeking more adventurous fishing venues. No longer content to fish their local rivers or reservoirs, fly fishermen are hunting further afield for species they may never have caught before. This edition, however, is devoted solely to flies used to catch the spotted denizen of rivers and still water, the trout.

Brown trout (*Salmo trutta*), originally a European and West Asian species, is found all over the world. The fish described by the Roman writer Claudius Aelianus in around A.D. 200 could well be the Brown trout. He describes the method of its capture in Macedonia with the use of an artificial fly; to date, this is the first written reference to fly-fishing in literature. The Brown trout has been introduced into the rivers of the U.S. and Canada, New Zealand, South Africa, Kenya, Zimbabwe, northern India, Sri Lanka, and Australia as well as waters in Chile and Argentina. In all these countries the Brown trout now breeds naturally and is thriving.

The other common species now introduced all over the world is the **Rainbow trout (*Oncorhynchus mykiss*).** This fish originates from the rivers of the western seaboard of the U.S. It thrives in the rivers of New Zealand, in particular, where there were no other fish in the rivers of any consequence except small fish, which are food for the introduced species. Rainbow trout is the main fish stocked in British

"put and take" fisheries due to its faster growth rate in the hatcheries; it is far cheaper to produce than the native Brown trout.

Other members of the salmon family called trout are not so well distributed worldwide as the Rainbow or Brown trout; nevertheless where they are found anglers with the artificial fly eagerly seek them. **Brook trout (*Salvelinus fontalis*)** is a species of trout, though is more accurately classified as a char. Sometimes called the Speckled trout, it is found in northern rivers of the U.S. and Canada; the record weight for this fish is over 14 lb.

Cutthroat trout (*Oncorhynchus clarki*), like Rainbow trout, is a creature from the western states of the U.S.; rivers such as the Yellowstone in Montana yield many fine specimens of this fish. The Cutthroat and Rainbow, when found in the same river system, can hybridize. **Dolly Varden (*Salvelinus malma*)** is another fish found in the U.S. and also in western Asia. It rarely grows over 18 in. except in the anadromous form (those fish that migrate up rivers to spawn) when it can grow to about 24 in.

Arctic char (*Salvelinus alpinus*) has the most northern distribution of any of the salmonids and is found in the Arctic, parts of northern Europe and even one or two lakes in the British Isles. **Lake trout (*Salvelinus namaycush*)** is another char from northern U.S. and northern Canada; it was found in large numbers in the Great Lakes. I have caught many fine specimens on my visits to Lake Kasba in the Northwest Territories of Canada—up to 25 lb. on an ultra large fly, but have caught many specimens of 6–7 lb. on nymph patterns in the Kazan River. The largest rod-caught 'Laker' in Canada weighed over 70 lb.

Throughout the world there are many species and localized variants of trout and char; in northern China, Manchuria, Mongolia, and North Korea, a species called the **Lenok trout (*Brachymystax lenok*)** is found. The **Marble trout (*Salmo trutta marmoratus*)** is found in the crystal waters of Slovenia. In Bosnia there is another unique species of trout called the **Soft Mouth trout (*Salmothymus obtusirostris*)** that looks like a Brown trout but has a head like a grayling.

There are species of trout peculiar to Lake Ohrid in Macedonia and also at least two species in Lake Baikal in Siberia. In some rivers in northern Turkey another sub-species of Brown trout is found which is peculiar to that country. There are also a number of localized strains and varieties of Rainbow trout—Golden trout and Apache trout are two such varieties. I mention these somewhat rare, esoteric fish because fly fishermen are venturing forth with their rods and flies to seek these remote spotted fish. Despite all the other species of fish now sought by today's fly fishermen, the trout in its many forms remains the supreme quarry for most of us.

dry flies

Dry flies, as the name indicates, are flies designed to be used on the surface of the water. They are created to imitate a wide variety of insects, which inhabit the surface of the water.

Newly hatched mayflies, floating on the surface to dry their wings before their first flight, are mimicked by a number of different artificial flies. This stage in the insect's life is known as the dun in angling parlance and, more scientifically, as the sub-imago. The female mayfly returning to the water to shed its eggs is known as a spinner; after laying its eggs and lying with wings outstretched in the surface film, it is referred to as a spent spinner or spent gnat. There are flies that emulate these two stages in the mayfly's life. Caddis or sedge flies with their roof-like wings, and stoneflies, one of the most primitive of aquatic insect forms, are also copied by the fly-dresser.

Apart from aquatic insects, many insects end up in or on the water by accident rather than design—they may be blown by the wind or fall off overhanging vegetation. They are known as "terrestrials" and form an important element of the trout diet. Beetles, grasshoppers, flies such as the black gnat, and even ants, are all trout fodder and receive attention at the fly-tying vice. Some dry flies are created with no particular insect in mind and are termed "fancy" or attractor flies, such as Wickham's Fancy on page 8.

On many rivers there is an all-important rule: "upstream dry fly" only. In the past, adherents to the discipline of the dry fly applied it to all trout fishing. However, most anglers on still waters in particular will fish the dry fly when required and will change to a wet fly or nymph as the conditions or the quarry dictate. Many dry flies are tied on up-eyed hooks, which have been manufactured solely for this purpose. However, it makes little difference whether the eye is up or down, provided the hook is fine enough. Nevertheless, some countries never resort to the up-eye for their dry-fly patterns. The illustrations here show dry flies tied on both up- and down-eyed hooks.

The patterns given in this section come from all corners of the fly-fishing world. Some have been employed for over a hundred years and are tied with traditional materials; others are more modern, utilizing man-made fibers and modern ingenuity.

Greenwell's Glory

This traditional fly has stood the test of time and is regarded as a classic. Devised by Canon William Greenwell and tied by James Wright, this fly is still used by anglers all over the fly-fishing world. It can represent many of the different species called olives.

Hook	12–16
Thread	Primrose
Tail	None (however, sometimes given a tail to aid floatability)
Body	Primrose tying silk well waxed to produce a shade of olive
Rib	Gold wire
Hackle	Greenwell (light furnace)
Wing	Blackbird substitute

Black Gnat

There are a number of natural flies covered by the term "black gnat." These insects are generally terrestrial flies of the Bibio species, though some anglers consider the water-loving Empid flies to be the true black gnat. Whichever the case, it does not alter the fact that the Black Gnat is found in the fly-boxes of most anglers.

Hook	12–16
Thread	Black
Tail	None (but like the Greenwell a tail is sometimes added)
Body	Black silk
Rib	Silver wire
Hackle	Black cock
Wing	Starling or gray duck

Wickham's Fancy

Another fly from gentler times that retains a degree of popularity. Wickham's Fancy does not represent any specific natural fly, but is a fancy dry fly. Though used extensively on rivers, a hackled version is used with some success by many British still-water anglers.

Hook	12–16
Thread	Brown
Tail	Ginger or light red cock hackle fibers
Body	Flat gold tinsel
Rib	Oval gold tinsel, wire in smaller sizes
Hackle	Ginger or light red cock, tied palmer-style
Wing	Gray duck

Blue-winged Olive

In nature, the blue-winged olive (*Ephemerella ignita*) is a widely distributed fly found on wild streams as well as on more sedate chalk streams. It is easily recognizable by its three tails (other olives have only two). This is an important fly pattern; the dressing given here is American in origin.

Hook	4–16
Thread	Olive
Tail	Dark dun hackle fibers
Body	Gray olive fur
Hackle	Dark dun cock
Wing	Dark blue dun hackle tips set upright

Olive Dun

The term "dun" is the fisherman's name for the first winged stage in an ephemerid's life. The more correct term is sub-imago. The artificial Olive Dun is a pattern that can imitate many of the natural olives. There are a number of different dressings for this fly.

Hook	12–14
Thread	Olive
Tail	Medium olive cock hackle fibers
Body	Cock hackle quill
Hackle	Medium olive cock
Wing	Gray starling

Dark Olive

The large dark olive (*Baetis rhodani*) is one of the commonest members of the Ephemeroptera (mayflies) of the British Isles. It is found in all parts of the U.K. and closely allied species are found throughout the U.S. and Europe. Good hatches can be expected early in the season with further hatches later in the year.

Hook	12–14
Thread	Olive
Tail	Dark olive cock hackle fibers
Body	Dyed olive goose herl
Rib	Fine gold wire
Hackle	Olive cock
Wing	Starling or gray duck

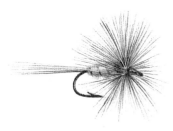

Rough Olive

A variation of the Dark Olive, there is little to choose between them. Both flies are considered excellent fish-takers by their respective adherents.

Hook	12–14
Thread	Olive
Tail	Brown olive cock hackle fibers
Body	Brown olive seal's fur
Rib	Gold wire
Hackle	Brown olive cock

Alder

The natural alder (*Sialis lutaria*) is on the wing in the U.K. during the months of May and June. Many eminent nineteenth-century writers wrote in fine praise of this artificial fly, but I must admit I have had very little success with it. However, I do know others who have taken better than normal trout on a dry Alder.

Hook	12
Thread	Black
Body	Magenta-dyed peacock herl
Hackle	Black cock
Wing	Mottled brown hen

Black Ant

This is a once-a-season fly, or twice if you are lucky. Flying ants fall onto the water in large numbers in late summer, exciting the trout to selective feeding. This pattern was devised by Barry Kent, an expert English fly-dresser who evolved this fly while living in South Africa. It has worked well for me on both river and still water, taking both trout and grayling. A red version can be tied using reddish brown suede chenille and a yellow version using cinnamon yellow suede chenille.

Hook	14–16
Thread	Black
Body	Black suede chenille
Hackle	A few fibers of cock pheasant tail, tied in the middle

Coch-y-Bonddu

The June bug, field chafer, and coch-y-bonddu are all names given to a little rotund beetle (*Phylopertha horticola*). As one of its common names implies, it is found in large numbers during the month of June and is in greatest evidence in the Celtic fringes of the British Isles. A few patterns of this fly are a must if you are fishing the wilder parts of the U.K. during the month of June.

Hook	12–14
Thread	Black
Body	Tip of flat gold tinsel, bronze peacock herl
Hackle	Dark furnace cock

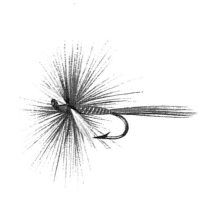

Lunn's Particular

The River Test of Hampshire is fabled for fish and fishing. W. J. Lunn was the keeper of the Houghton Club stretch for 45 years, caring for his river from 1887. The care of the stream was in the hands of the Lunn family for many years, creating an unbroken tradition. This fly is his creation and first saw the light of day around 1916; it has continued to catch fish since that time. A classic fly in all senses of the word, it is a good imitation of the olive spinner.

Hook	14
Thread	Brown
Tail	Natural red cock hackle fibers
Body	Undyed stalk of a Rhode Island Red cock hackle
Hackle	Natural red cock
Wing	Two medium dun cock hackle points, tied spent

Cranefly

A large number of the family Tipulidae are terrestrial insects. However, a fair proportion are aquatic and their larval and pupal stages are spent in water. Both types are taken readily by trout. Late-season fishing on the large reservoirs with the floating daddy-longlegs is perhaps one of the highlights of the angling calendar. There are many artificials tied to imitate this fly, but this particular one has proved to be constantly effective.

Hook	Standard size 10 or long shank 12
Thread	Black or brown
Body	Cock pheasant tail fibers
Rib	Fluorescent green floss
Hackle	Natural red or cree cock
Wing	Cree hackle points
Legs	Cock pheasant tail fibers, knotted

Gray Duster

This fly can best be described as a broad-spectrum dry pattern, imitating nothing specific and yet imitating whatever the trout thinks it is. There are some who maintain that it is a fair representation of a moth of sorts. Others believe that it is effective during a rise of chironomid midges. The Gray Duster is a killing fly for both running and still waters.

Hook	12–16
Thread	Black or brown
Body	Rabbit fur mixed with the blue underfur
Hackle	Well-marked badger

Sherry Spinner

This fly is tied to imitate the egg-laying stage of the blue-winged olive. Some prefer this pattern to the Orange Quill (overleaf). A well-known brand of sherry owes its name to this fly, or perhaps it is the other way around.

Hook	14
Thread	Brown (light)
Tail	Honey dun cock hackle fibers
Body	Sherry-colored floss, or a mixture of seal's fur to give sherry color
Rib	Fine gold wire
Hackle	Honey dun cock
Wing	Optional: two blue dun hackle points tied spent

Orange Quill

This fly is the creation of the famed father of English nymph fishing, G.E.M. Skues, who fished well into his eighties on the chalk streams of Hampshire. He questioned and antagonized many of the dry-fly-only dogmatists of his time. Although he was a controversial figure in his day, he was respected by all, even though he must have seemed a heretic to many. He found this particular dry fly to be extremely effective when the blue-winged olive was on the water.

Hook	14
Thread	Hot orange
Tail	Natural red cock hackle fibers
Body	Orange quill; the original called for condor, ostrich is acceptable
Hackle	Natural dark red cock
Wing	Pale starling

Ginger Quill

This is a favorite fly of many anglers, used on West Country (U.K.) rivers. It is thought to imitate such insects as the pale wateries and other medium olives.

Hook	12–16
Thread	Black or brown
Tail	Ginger cock hackle fibers
Body	Stripped peacock quill from the eye of the feather
Hackle	Ginger cock
Wing	Gray starling

Gold-ribbed Hare's Ear (GRHE)

This is one of my favorite flies and appears in my fly-box for any corner of the world. Though the pattern depicted is for a dry fly, it can be fished wet or as a nymph. It can be very effective fished on the surface film as a stillborn olive. On British reservoirs long-shanked, weighted versions have proved very successful for both Rainbow and Brown trout. An American nymph pattern appears on page 102.

Hook	12–14
Thread	Black or brown
Tail	Guard hair fibers from a hare's face
Body	Hare's ear
Rib	Gold wire
Hackle	Fibers picked out to form the hackle
Wing	None (sometimes a gray starling wing is added)

Blue Dun

This is a fly with a long lineage going back to the time of Charles Cotton. Each part of the British Isles has its Blue Dun pattern, some winged, some hackled, some wet, some only fished dry. It is not really certain what natural insect the Blue Dun imitates. It is probably yet another fly that represents the large dark olive.

Hook	14
Thread	Primrose
Tail	Blue dun cock hackle fibers
Body	Mole fur
Hackle	Blue dun cock
Wing	Gray starling

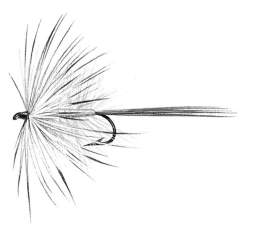

French Partridge Mayfly

There are a number of different dressings of this fly, but all of them use the barred hackle from a French partridge. This fly is one of my favorites.

Hook	Long shank 12
Thread	Black or brown
Tail	Cock pheasant tail fibers
Body	Natural raffia
Rib	Gold wire
Hackle	Palmered olive cock down the body, French partridge feather at the head

Gray Drake

The term "drake" originates from the feathers used in the wing of this fly. It is tied in the style termed "fanwing," which is self-explanatory. Though looking realistic to the angler's eye, there is a hardening of opinion in the U.K. against this style of Mayfly. Though I prefer the hackled type of fly, there are still many who swear by this style of dressing.

Hook	Long shank 12
Thread	Black or brown
Tail	Fibers from a cock pheasant tail
Body	Natural raffia or white silk
Rib	Black silk
Hackle	Badger
Wing	Gray duck body feathers, tied fanwing

Green Drake

An olive version of the Gray Drake. It is thought that the Gray Drake represents the female dun of *Ephemera danica* and the Green Drake the male of that species.

Hook	Long shank 12
Thread	Olive
Tail	Cock pheasant tail fibers
Body	Olive floss
Rib	Gold wire
Hackle	Olive cock
Wing	Duck breast feathers dyed olive, tied fanwing

Yellow Drake

Follow the pattern above but use an overall yellow color.

Shadow Mayfly

This fly is the creation of Peter Deane, one of Britain's leading fly-dressers. It is a very impressionistic pattern that catches a lot of fish on the Hampshire chalk streams. It has also been used as a dapping fly.

Hook	Long shank 10–12
Thread	Black
Body	None as such; the hackle provides the body
Hackle	Palmered grizzle cock
Wing	Ginger hackle tips clipped at the top

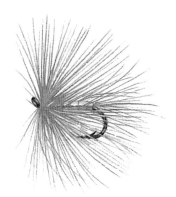

Hawthorn

Sometimes spelt Hawthorne, this fly is based on the insect *Bibio marci*. "Marci" comes from the fact that it was supposed to hatch out on or around St. Mark's day. This terrestrial fly is an essential pattern for the month of May in most parts of the U.K. When the hawthorn blossom is out, you usually find the hawthorn fly on the wing.

Hook	10–14
Thread	Black
Body	Black-dyed goose fibers
Rib	None (some patterns use fine silver wire)
Hackle	Black cock
Wing	Gray duck
Legs	Two feather strands left trailing

Orange and Gold

I was first shown this fly by one of the anglers who fish those large Midland reservoirs, Grafham and Rutland in the UK. It is particularly effective when trout are feeding on floating snails. The color orange perhaps emulates the reddish-orange color that shows through the infant snail's shell when viewed against the light. This color is caused by the hemoglobin present in many of the pulmonate snails.

Hook	12–14
Thread	Brown or orange
Body	Flat gold lurex
Hackle	Palmered orange-dyed cock

Walker's Sedge

This large fly is tied to represent the large red sedge and other large caddis flies. The addition of a small butt of fluorescent wool or silk at the tail end of the fly enhances its killing properties. There are a further two flies in Richard Walker's Mayfly series: one using a green front hackle and another using a hackle of brown-dyed speckled duck feathers.

Hook	8–10
Thread	Black
Body	First a small tag of fluorescent arc chrome wool, then ostrich herl (chestnut color, clipped short)
Hackle	Two natural red cock
Wing	A bunch of natural red cock hackle fibers

Cinnamon Sedge

One of the most popular of the sedge or caddis fly patterns, this artificial can imitate a number of light brown sedges apart from the actual cinnamon sedge (*Limnephilus lunatus*). It emerges in June and is found in quite large numbers flying at dusk or late afternoon.

Hook	10–12
Thread	Brown
Body	Cinnamon turkey herl
Rib	Gold wire (optional)
Hackle	Light ginger cock
Wing	Cinnamon hen or turkey wing quill

Welsh Partridge

This can be used as a wet or dry fly and can well represent the natural claret dun (*Leptophlebia vespertina*). It can also work well as an imitation of the march brown. The fly was created by Courtney Williams, author of *A Dictionary of Trout Flies* and of *Flies for Seatrout and Grayling*.

Hook	12–16
Thread	Black
Tail	Two strands from a partridge tail
Body	Claret seal's fur
Rib	Fine gold oval
Hackle	Stiff claret cock with brown partridge in front

Bumble Bee

There are times when, no matter what fly we use, we cannot seem to tempt the trout to take. In these situations, large, incongruous flies like the Bumble Bee defy all reason and cause the fish to take. Many times I have seen trout rise and take natural bumble bees when they have fallen on the water. This fly was devised by the late Richard Walker.

Hook	6
Thread	Black
Body	White, black, and amber ostrich herl
Wing	Grizzle hackle points
Thorax	Black ostrich herl
Legs	Black cock pheasant tail fibers, knotted

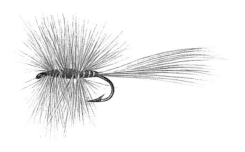

Blue Upright

A favorite fly from the county of Devon in the U.K., the Blue Upright was created by R.S. Austin, famous for the Tup's Indispensable (see page 24). This fly is a good floater for the rough streams as the hackle extends from the shoulder to the eye.

Hook	10–14
Thread	Purple
Tail	Steely blue cock hackle fibers
Body	Undyed peacock herl, stripped
Hackle	Steely blue cock

Imperial

This fly is sometimes called the Kite's Imperial after its originator, the late Major Oliver Kite. It is used as an imitation of the dark olive (*Baetis rhodani*). Oliver Kite died in 1968 while on a fishing trip.

Hook	14–16
Thread	Purple
Tail	Grayish brown in early season; later, honey cock hackle fibers
Body	Heron primary herl doubled to form a thorax
Rib	Fine gold wire
Hackle	Honey dun cock

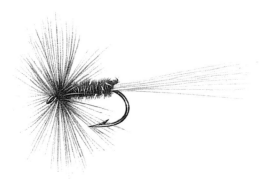

Pheasant Tail

The chestnut brown herls from the center tail of a cock pheasant provide the fly-tier with a material that is known for its versatility. Used for both nymphs and dry flies, it is a fly-dressing medium I could not be without. The dry Pheasant Tail is a pattern from Devon (U.K.), where it is still considered to be one of the finest. The dressing given was one of Skue's patterns.

Hook	12–16
Thread	Black or sometimes yellow
Tail	Cock pheasant tail fibers or honey dun cock fibers
Body	Dark red cock pheasant tail fibers
Rib	Gold wire
Hackle	Honey dun cock

Beacon Beige

This is another fly, based on the earlier Devon fly, from the vice of Peter Deane. He named this pattern after the hill Culmstock Beacon, which dominates the valley of the River Culm. This is a good fly with excellent floating properties and a high degree of visibility.

Hook	14–16
Thread	Brown
Tail	Grizzle cock hackle fibers
Body	Stripped peacock quill from the eye of the feather
Hackle	Grizzle cock and natural red game

Terry's Terror

This dry fly was conjured up by Ernest Lock of Andover and his angling friend Dr. C. Terry of Bath. It is a good fish taker when olives are on the water, although it certainly does not look anything like the natural olive. It is just one of those flies that works.

Hook	10–16
Thread	Black or brown
Tail	Equal parts of yellow and orange goat hair clipped short and flared
Body	Peacock herl
Rib	Fine copper tinsel
Hackle	Natural red cock

Goddard's Caddis

Sometimes called the G & H Sedge, this fly was devised by John Goddard and Cliff Henry at Bough Beech reservoir in Kent, where they both fished. This fly can imitate a wide range of larger sedge flies and is unique in its wing construction, using buoyant deer hair clipped to a wing shape. This pattern has achieved wide popularity on both sides of the Atlantic.

Hook	Long shank 12–14
Thread	Black
Body	Underbody green or yellow wool
Hackle	Two light red cock hackles clipped at the top, stalks left uncut to form antennae
Wing	Spun deer hair cut to shape

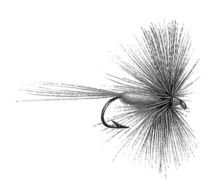

Dark Cahill

This fly can imitate a wide number of indigenous mayflies. *Hexagenia atrocaudata*, which hatches from many of the eastern rivers of the U.S., is among them.

Hook	12–16
Thread	Brown
Tail	Brown hackle fibers
Body	Fine brown fur
Hackle	Medium red cock
Wing	Wood duck fibers

Tup's Indispensable

Tup is a country name for a ram and this fly was so named because the thorax was made up of wool from the hair on the scrotum of a ram, as well as cream seal's fur and lemon spaniel's hair. The originator of this fly was R.S. Austin, the Devonshire fly-dresser. On the advice of Skues, who rated this fly highly, crimson seal's fur was later added to the thorax, giving it a pinkish tinge. I have found this fly to be successful when pale wateries are on the river.

Hook	14–16
Thread	Yellow
Tail	Honey dun cock fibers
Body	Two-thirds yellow floss, one-third "tup's" mixture
Hackle	Honey dun cock

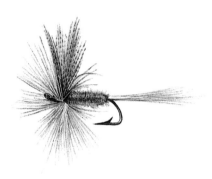

Light Hendrikson

Another famous standard American dry-fly pattern, this is intended to represent the mayfly or at least the female of the species.

Hook	12–14
Thread	Brown
Tail	Medium dun hackle fibers
Body	Pale pinkish-brown fox fur or synthetic substitute
Hackle	Medium dun cock
Wing	Wood duck fibers

Dark Hendrikson

As its name suggests, this is a darker version of the previous Hendrikson fly. Originated by Ron Steenrod around 1915, the Hendrikson was named after one of his best customers. The Dark Hendrikson came after the light one.

Hook	12–18
Thread	Gray
Tail	Dark dun cock hackle fibers
Body	Dark muskrat or synthetic substitute
Hackle	Dark dun cock
Wing	Wood duck fibers

Quill Gordon

A fly named after the father of American dry-fly fishing Theodore Gordon. It was first used in the 1890s on the streams of the Catskills. Gordon corresponded regularly with his counterparts in the U.K., Skues amongst them.

Hook	12–18
Thread	Cream or light brown
Tail	Medium dun cock hackle fibers
Body	Stripped peacock quill
Rib	Fine gold wire (optional)
Hackle	Medium dun cock
Wing	Wood duck

Adams

A favorite pattern of mine since a day on the River Itchen when I made short work of about 12 Brown trout that took my size 16 Adams for a medium olive. Since then I have always included this American classic fly in my fly-box. The fly originated from Michigan in the early 1920s.

Hook	10–20
Thread	Gray or black
Tail	Mixed brown and grizzle cock hackle fibers
Body	Muskrat
Hackle	Mixed brown and grizzle cock
Wing	Grizzle cock hackle tips

Humpy

This fly from the fast-flowing rivers in western U.S. is sometimes called the Goofus Bug. A number of body colors are used, especially yellow, red, olive, and orange. The underbody of the original Humpy was made from the tying thread. More modern ties tend to use a synthetic fur or antron dubbing.

Hook	10–14
Thread	Yellow
Tail	Moose body hair
Body	Natural deer hair over an abdomen of dubbed synthetic light yellow fur
Hackle	Grizzle cock
Wing	Tips of the deer hair that was used as the body medium

King River Caddis

A traditional-style caddis fly originated by American fly-tier Bus Buszek. Though modern styles of caddis patterns are now freely available, this conventional dry sedge still maintains a high degree of popularity.

Hook	10–16
Thread	Black
Body	Light brown synthetic fur
Hackle	Brown cock
Wing	Mottled turkey

Royal Wulff

This fly is based on the well-known standard pattern, the Royal Coachman, with a peacock herl and red silk body. Like most of the flies in the Wulff series, it is sometimes used for salmon.

Hook	8–14
Thread	Black
Tail	Natural deer hair
Body	Peacock herl with red floss center
Hackle	Brown cock
Wing	White calf tail

Elk Hair Caddis

The use of deer or elk body hair as a winging medium for caddis fly imitations is now well established on both sides of the Atlantic. Terry Thomas in the U.K. created a fly that he called the Dark Sedge using deer body hair for the wing. The pattern given here was devised by Al Troth and is used in the American northwest with a great deal of success.

Hook	10–14
Thread	Brown
Body	Olive synthetic dubbing
Hackle	Brown palmered cock
Wing	Natural elk hair, the butts extended to form the head

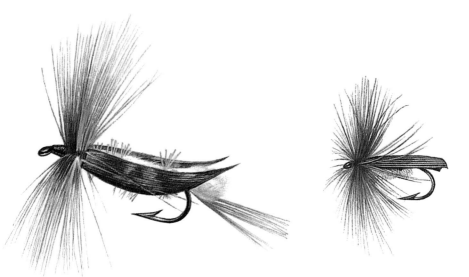

Joe's Hopper

One of the many American patterns devised to imitate the terrestrial grasshopper. I have used this fly as a large caddis imitation on British reservoirs.

Hook	Long shank 14–18
Thread	Black or brown
Tail	Red hackle fibers plus a loop of yellow wool
Body	Yellow wool
Rib	Palmered natural red cock, clipped short
Hackle	Natural red cock
Wing	Two strips of mottled turkey wing flanking the body

Dean's Grasshopper

A New Zealand pattern of long standing, the Grasshopper has figured in the fly wallets of fishermen since the days of Charles Cotton (1630–1687). Live grasshoppers are sometimes used as dapping flies on some of the Irish lakes.

Hook	10–12
Thread	Brown
Body	Straw-colored cock hackles wound palmer-style and clipped
Hackle	Brown cock
Wing	Black feather, varnished and clipped in half moon

Brandon's Claret

This is a fancy dry fly from Australia. The three cock hackles at the head ensure that this fly is, at the very least, a good floater.

Hook	10–12
Thread	Black
Tail	Golden pheasant tippet fibers
Body	Fat claret seal's fur or mohair
Rib	Oval gold tinsel
Hackle	Three black cock

Shoo Fly

This is a fancy pattern from New Zealand for use on still waters. The original winging medium called for a veined plastic, but the pattern shown here uses raffene (Swiss straw).

Hook	10–14
Thread	Black
Tail	Scarlet cock
Body	Peacock herl
Hackle	Rhode Island Red
Wing	Raffene

Tri-tree Beetle

This is a typical terrestrial pattern imitating one of the indigenous Australian beetles. Every fly-fishing country has its own beetle patterns and Australia is no exception. This pattern can be fished wet or dry.

Hook	10–12
Thread	Black
Body	Black ostrich herl
Hackle	Black cock
Wing case	Brown feather tied over the back

Mooi Moth

Most South African dry flies are derived from or are actual British flies. However, this pattern, the Mooi Moth, is purebred South African.

Hook	10–12
Thread	Black
Tail	Medium blue dun cock hackle fibers
Body	Stripped peacock quill from the eye
Hackle	Medium blue dun cock
Wing	Gray duck

Diabolo

This is a French pattern for rough water. The fore-and-aft hackle helps its floating potential. This fly is the creation of Guy Plas of Marcillac-la-Croisille. There are a number of color variations for the body: yellow, olive, gray, and the red version depicted here.

Hook	12–16
Thread	Black or red
Body	Red silk, varnished
Hackle	Blue dun cock (dark) fore-and-aft

Tricolore

This pattern is a French palmered fly and is used for both trout and grayling throughout Europe.

Hook	12–14
Thread	Black
Tail	Light ginger cock hackle fibers
Hackle	Three: black, ginger, and blue dun cock (there are other color combinations)

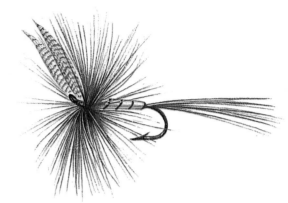

Fourmi Brun

A favorite fly of the late Charles Ritz, one of France's greatest fly fishermen as well as a leading hotelier. The time to use the ant in Europe is late summer.

Hook	12–16
Thread	Black or brown
Body	Peacock herl/orange floss/cock pheasant tail fibers
Hackle	Natural red cock
Wing	Blue dun cock hackle tips set over the back

Pont Audemer

A traditional fly from Normandy, there are a number of variations of Pont Audemer. All are used from May onward on the chalk streams of that area.

Hook	10–14
Thread	Black
Tail	Red cock hackle fibers, or cock pheasant tail fibers
Body	Natural raffia
Rib	Black silk
Hackle	Two medium natural red cock
Wing	Gray speckled duck tied over the eye

Favourite de Carrére

This fly could be described as a French
version of the Red Tag, one of the
standard old-time flies originating in
Worcestershire in the U.K. The Favourite
de Carrére is used for both trout and
grayling and can be fished wet or dry.

Hook	10–14
Thread	Black
Body	Peacock herl with a red silk tip
Hackle	Natural red cock

L'Olive Moyenne

This pattern is one of a series of flies
known as the Gallica series—I believe
this one to be number 9. It is an
imitation of the medium olive. The
original dressing called for a dyed natural
raffia body, although a PVC material has
been used for the example shown here.

Hook	12–14
Thread	Olive
Tail	Blue dun hackle fibers
Body	Thin brown PVC
Rib	Yellow silk
Hackle	Brownish olive with blue dun cock in front
Wing	Two blue dun cock hackle tips with a mauvish tinge

Panama

This is a popular pattern in France. In the past years I have been asked to tie quite a number of these flies for British anglers. The fly can best be described as a fancy dry pattern.

Hook	10–14
Thread	Black
Tail	Golden pheasant tippet
Body	Natural raffia tipped with four turns of black silk
Rib	Palmered (natural) red cock
Hackle	Natural red cock; front hackle brown partridge
Wing	Cree hackle points

Victor's Sedge

I obtained this fly from Victor Salt of Madrid who based his pattern on a French type of fly. The hackles come from the fabled cocks of Leon, world-renowned for the quality of their shiny, stiff feathers.

Hook	10–14
Thread	Brown
Body	Cock pheasant tail fibers
Hackle	Natural red cock
Wing	Mottled fibers from the spade hackle (Flor de Escoba)

Roman Moser Sedge

Like many modern caddis/sedge patterns, this one from the Moser stable also uses the good floating properties of deer body hair for the body, legs, and head.

Hook	8–12
Thread	Brown
Body	Deer hair bound lengthwise along the hook
Hackle	Collar of deer hair
Wing	Preformed sedge wing
Head	Deer hair

Roman Moser Stonefly

Like his dun pattern, Moser's stonefly imitation also uses modern synthetic materials to achieve a most realistic fly. Roman Moser's flies are almost too good to fish with.

Hook	Long shank 8–14
Thread	Brown
Body	Thin foam plastic, yellow color
Hackle	Palmered blue dun cock, with a deer hair collar to simulate legs
Wing	Special preformed stonefly wing
Head	Thin gray plastic foam rubber

Roman Moser Dun

N.E. Sedge

One of the most realistic dry olive dun patterns I have ever seen, this fly, tied by one of Austria's leading fly-dressers, uses up-to-the-minute materials. The interesting feature of this fly is the wing, which is preformed. Most Roman Moser flies use man-made products in their construction, available from the fly-dressing house Traun River Products.

This typical Austrian sedge was devised by Norbert Eipeltauer of Vienna. Sedge flies are used on many of the Austrian mountain streams.

Hook	10–14
Thread	Black
Body	Brown or olive nylon dubbing
Hackle	Palmered brown cock
Wing	Hen pheasant

Hook	12–14
Thread	Yellow
Tail	Light ginger cock hackle fibers
Body	Yellow or olive poly dubbing
Hackle	Light ginger cock, palmered down the body, then clipped underneath
Wing	Preformed wing manufactured for this purpose

Mayfly

The natural mayfly occurs on many of the slower-running rivers of Austria during May and June. This pattern uses a preformed detached latex body, which not only looks realistic, but also helps the fly to float well.

Hook	10–12
Thread	Black or brown
Tail	Three cock pheasant tail feathers
Body	Preformed detached latex
Hackle	Olive cock
Wing	Mallard breast feathers dyed yellow, olive, or natural

White Moth

This Austrian pattern is sometimes called the White Sedge and is a good fly for both trout and grayling, especially at dusk.

Hook	12–16
Thread	Black
Body	White nylon or poly dubbing
Hackle	Palmered white cock
Wing	White duck or goose

Chochin

This small fly by Luis Antunez Jr. of Madrid, represents a wide number of small Diptera species that get caught in the surface film. This is termed a fore-and-aft fly, having a hackle at either end which enhances the floating potential of the fly.

Hook	14–16
Thread	Olive
Body	Flat gold tinsel with clear green Swannundaze over
Hackle	Tail hackle pale blue dun cock; head hackle dark blue dun cock
Thorax	Brown synthetic fur

Hoz Seca

Another ephemerid-imitating pattern from Luis Antunez. Seca means dry and Hoz can mean a sickle or a ravine; in this case it is the name of a river.

Hook	14
Thread	Light brown
Tail	Medium blue dun cock
Body	Dirty olive synthetic fur
Rib	Close turns of fine copper wire
Hackle	Blue dun and light red cock, mixed
Wing	Dirty gray polypropylene

Verano Amarillo

Tajo

The Yellow Summer is another fly created by Luis Antunez, a fly-dresser of great skill and ingenuity. This fly imitates one of the summer olives.

Hook	12–14
Thread	Primrose
Tail	Medium blue dun cock
Body	Two-thirds yellow goose or swan fiber, one-third green fiber
Hackle	Medium blue dun cock

This dry fly is named after the famous river of Spain and Portugal, the Tagus, which flows into the sea at Lisbon. Like the other Spanish flies, Hoz Seca and Verano Amarillo, this is a representation of a mayfly.

Hook	14–16
Thread	Primrose
Tail	Medium blue dun cock
Body	Varnished orange silk with a tip of dark gray
Hackle	Blue dun cock
Wing	Gray polypropylene

Moustique 1

This Swiss fly is a representation of some of the smaller, pale-colored ephemerids, the equivalent perhaps of the British species the pale watery (*Baetis bioculatus*) or even the small spurwing (*Centroptilum luteolum*).

Hook	14–16
Thread	Black or brown
Tail	Medium blue dun cock hackle fibers
Body	Yellow floss silk
Hackle	Feather from a duck's green preen gland, clipped to size
Wing	Two blue dun cock hackle tips

Universal Sedge 1

This Swiss caddis pattern is one of a series using different colored bodies to imitate a wide range of natural caddis flies. They can best be described as a broad-spectrum fly. The wings of the Universal series are tied flat along the body. The two slips of feather are tied one on top of the other, forming the distinctive "V" at the rear. Examples of these flies in my collection have lacquered wings to give additional strength to the fly.

Hook	10–12
Thread	Black
Body	Light green PVC strip
Hackle	Natural red cock with white cock in front
Wing	Hen pheasant wing quill, tied flat on top

The "F" Fly

This particular pattern was created by Marjan Fratnik of Milan (formally of Most Na Soci in Slovenia). He was acquainted with the Moustique series of flies from the Swiss Jura. However, as good as they are, Marjan thought they were a little fragile and he developed his "F" Fly. This unique dry fly, using the feathers from the duck's preen gland, has been tested by fly fishermen all over Europe and found to be a most killing pattern. It is used for both trout and grayling.

Hook	10–18
Thread	Black, gray, olive, or yellow
Body	Tying thread or heron herl
Hackle/ wing	Combined hackle and wing from a small duck gland feather

The Grouse Wing

This is one of a series of sedge flies developed by Dr. Bozidar Voljc after an extensive study of the sedges of the Slovenian mountain and chalk streams. One of the most unique factors of Dr. Voljc's flies is their almost indestructible nature, which is due in the main to his method of winging. The wings are prepared by coating the feather with PVC glue and sticking it to nonelastic nylon, which gives strength to the fly.

Hook	14
Thread	Black
Body	Palmered dark ginger cock
Hackle	Dark ginger cock
Wing	Woodcock body feather glued to nylon

The Caperer

The Caperer is another excellent sedge
fly in the series developed by Dr. Bozidar
Voljc. The design is very hardwearing
and is made in the same way as
described opposite.

Hook	Long shank 8
Thread	Black
Body	Palmered dark cream badger
Hackle	Dark cream badger or greenwell cock
Wing	Cock pheasant flank glued to nylon

Yellow Sally

This fly is part of the Carniolica series,
developed by Dr. Bozidar Voljc. The
Alpine rivers of Slovenia are rich in many
species of stoneflies and Dr. Voljc has
sought to imitate many of these stoneflies.

Hook	14–18
Thread	Yellow
Body	Palmered, dyed yellow cock hackle
Hackle	Yellow cock
Wing	Yellow cock hackle treated with a PVC adhesive and trimmed to shape

The Willow Fly

This European species is classed as a
medium to small stonefly and is found in
most parts of the U.K. except the eastern
counties. It appears in late August
through to the end of November. This
species favors clean rivers and streams
with gravel bottoms. Its scientific name is
Leuctra geniculata. This pattern is one in
the Carniolica series created for Slovenian
rivers by Dr. Bozidar Voljc.

Hook	14
Thread	Black
Body	Palmered medium blue dun cock
Hackle	Medium blue dun cock
Wing	Medium blue dun cock treated with PVC adhesive

The Large Stonefly

This species (*Perla bipunctata*) hatches
in May and June. It is one of the largest
species in the U.K. and can be found in
the north of England and the West
Country. It is a creature of the fast
flowing spate rivers and also of the crystal
karst streams of Slovenia. This is another
pattern in the Carniolica series by Dr.
Bozidar Voljc.

Hook	Long shank 12
Thread	Black
Body	Yellow polypropylene, palmered with medium blue dun cock hackle
Hackle	Medium blue dun cock
Wing	Medium blue dun cock treated with PVC adhesive

Hornberg

The Hornberg is a most unusual pattern, sometimes called the Hornberg Special Streamer. It was created by Frank Hornberg of Wisconsin, U.S. It is a popular pattern throughout the U.S. and Canada, where it has many adherents in Quebec. It is used as a dry-sedge pattern, but it is one of those flies that when it sinks is then fished as a wet fly.

Hook	Long shank 8–12
Thread	Black
Body	Flat silver tinsel
Hackle	Two grizzle cock
Wing	Yellow cock hackle fibers, flanked by gray mottled mallard flank. The tips of the mallard feather are varnished together
Cheeks	Jungle cock (optional)

Renegade

This dry fly can be used on both river and lake. It is considered an excellent pattern for Cutthroat trout. It was devised in Wyoming by Taylor "Beartracks" Williams in the late 1920s and since that time has been used throughout the Pacific northwest right up into Alaska.

Hook	8–14
Thread	Black
Tip	Flat gold tinsel
Body	Peacock herl
Hackle	Rear hackle brown cock; front hackle white cock

Hawthorn X

The natural hawthorn (*Bibio marci*) is
a very important fly on rivers and still
waters during May when large numbers
swarm near the hawthorn blossom; they
are weak fliers and often fall onto the
water where they are eaten by fish. See
also page 18 for the Hawthorn.

Hook	Down-eyed 10–12
Thread	Black
Body	Fine black dubbing
Wing	A short tuft of white calf and a few fibers of pearl tinsel
Thorax/ head	Black deer hair tied over the eye of the hook, brought back bullet-style and then tied down
Legs	Rubber hackle tied at the sides: short in the front, longer at the back to imitate the trailing legs of the natural

Twilight Beauty

This is a very popular New Zealand
pattern tied to imitate the natural insect
Oniscigaster distans or *O. wakefieldi*, a
dark species of mayfly fairly common
throughout New Zealand.

Hook	Down-eyed 12–14
Thread	Black
Tail	Medium red cock hackle fibers
Body	Black or dark brown tying silk
Hackle	Mixed dark brown and black cock wound together
Wing	Dark gray, almost black duck quill set upright

Parachute Hopper

A pattern from the U.S. that represents those lumbering terrestrials that end up in the watery world of the trout. This particular dressing uses a parachute hackle rather than the more conventional ties.

Hook	Long shank 8–14
Thread	Brown
Body	Light tan dubbing
Rib	Very fine copper wire
Hackle	Grizzle cock
Wing	Pale ginger feather fiber treated with a fixative for durability
Thorax	As body
Post	White calf; this also acts as a sight indicator for the fisherman
Legs	Knotted cock pheasant tail fibers

Madam X

A fairly recent pattern devised by Doug Swisher and used to great effect as a searching fly on Montana's rivers and streams. I also saw it in use on the Snake River in Wyoming. This pattern was the forerunner of other similar flies such as the Hawthorn X (see opposite).

Hook	Long shank 8–14
Thread	Black or brown
Tail	Natural deer hair
Body	Fluorescent yellow or orange silk
Wing and head	Natural deer hair tied bullet-style, first tied over the hook then brought back and tied down
Legs	White rubber hackles

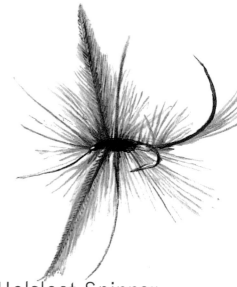

Mottled Sedge

This caddis pattern comes from the Czech Republic where there is a thriving interest in fly-fishing. The Czech tyers are very innovative; take, for example, the dubbing wicks or dubbing brushes available in many fly-tying catalogues— these were originally a Czech creation. As are many of the glass eyes used on some of our large flies.

Hook	Down-eyed 10–14
Thread	Black or yellow
Body	Pale yellow fur dubbing
Hackle	Palmered ginger cock
Front hackle	Dark ginger or light red cock
Wing	Two feather strips of turkey or pheasant, pretreated with fixative and laid crossing one on top of the other, forming a "V" at the rear

Holsloot Spinner

A Tony Biggs pattern named after the Holsloot River in Western Cape, South Africa; I fished this river a few years ago, but kept looking over my shoulder all the time for I had seen the imprint of a leopard's paw in the sand by the side of the stream. It was very difficult to concentrate in the circumstances!

Hook	Down-eyed 10–14
Thread	Black
Tail	Blue dun cock hackle fibers
Body	Dark heron or blue crane feather herl
Hackle	Dark blue dun cock
Wing	Dark blue hackle points tied spent
Legs	A few strands of fine peacock herl splayed around the shank like the R.A.B. (see opposite)
Antennae	Hackle stalks from the hackles (optional)

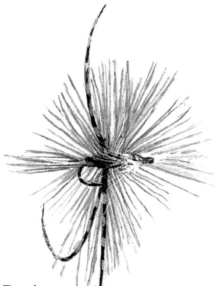

Red-arsed Bastard

The Red-arsed Bastard, or R.A.B., was created by the South African fisherman Mark Mackereth. It was popularized and further developed by Tony Biggs of Cape Town, who uses this pattern on some of the clear, thin waters of the Western Cape where the fish can be difficult.

Hook	Down-eyed 10–14
Thread	Red
Tip	A few turns of the tying thread exposed at the end
Body	Three or four cock pheasant tail fibers tied in at the butt end and wound up the shank to about half-way; the fine ends are not cut off but allowed to splay around the hook shank. Alternatively, try using a few strands of fine peacock herl tips
Hackle	Natural red cock

Willow Grub

This is one of the most simple yet effective patterns on the Mataura River in South Island, New Zealand. It is tied to imitate the small caterpillar of the sawfly *Pontania proxima*. Large Brown trout lurk under the overhanging willows on this river and readily accept willow grubs if they happen to fall into the stream or even let themselves down into the water accidentally as they are prone to doing.

Hook	14–16
Thread	Brown
Body	Fine cream dubbing with no guard hairs
Head	Built up to a round button with the tying thread

Steindorfer's Burzell

A Bavarian pattern that makes use of the cul-de-canard (preen feather) for the wing. This pattern was a prize-winner for Werner Steindorfer at a big fly-tying competition during the Fly Fair at Ljubljana in Slovenia some years ago.

Hook	Down-eyed 12–16
Thread	Black
Tail	Two fine cock pheasant tail fibers
Body	Stripped peacock quill
Wing	Cul-de-canard, two bunches, short clipped at the rear, blending with two larger at the front
Thorax	White foam pad

Green Body Sedge

This modern caddis pattern was devised by the innovative Dutch tier Hans Van Klinken; it is equally good for grayling as it is for trout. This fly also makes a good imitation of a green gauze wing, a terrestrial that sometimes interests the trout.

Hook	Down-eyed 10–16
Thread	Brown
Body	Pale yellow dubbing with the back marked fluorescent green
Hackle	Short grizzle cock
Wing	White transparent plastic cut to shape
Thorax	Thin peacock herl

Loop Wing Snipe Fly

This pattern comes from South Africa and was sent to me by Ed Herbst of Cape Town. The snipe fly (*Atherix androgyna*) is a very common insect on many South African waters. The females lay their eggs on streamside rocks then expire, falling into the water to provide the trout with an easy meal.

Hook	Down-eyed 12–14
Thread	Yellow
Body	A mix of yellow seal's fur and yellow Haretron
Hackle	Short-fibered cree cock
Loop wings	Fine antron and gray crystal flash wound together and formed into a loop either side of the body
Thorax	A strand of peacock herl

Swiss Grasshopper

Most countries have their hopper patterns and there are a number of examples in this book. This simple pattern comes from Switzerland where, in summer, alpine meadows vibrate to the song of countless grasshoppers.

Hook	Long shank 8–14
Thread	Olive
Body	Olive yarn, with a strip of white yarn tied in underneath
Rib	Yellow thread
Wing	Gray duck wing strips
Legs	Knotted cock pheasant tail fibers

Shuttlecock

An emerger pattern used on waters such as the famous West Country reservoirs Chew and Blagdon in the U.K., it was popularized by one of the leading match fishermen of that area, Bev Perkins. It represents, like the Shipman's Buzzer, an emerging chironomid midge.

Hook	Down-eyed 10–16
Thread	To match the body color
Tail	Fluorescent red, orange, or signal green silk
Body	Feather fibre, i.e. pheasant tail, heron herl
Rib	Very fine copper wire (optional)
Wing	Cul-de-canard-like shuttlecock over the eye
Thorax	As body

Shipman's Buzzer

This pattern imitates another emerging chironomid midge. Though created in 1979–80 by Dave Shipman, it has become very popular in recent years with British still-water anglers. It can come in a variety of body colors.

Hook	Down-eyed 10–16
Thread	To match the body
Tail and head filaments	White antron
Body	Olive, orange, gray, black, fiery brown, and green seal's fur or substitute
Rib	Flat gold tinsel

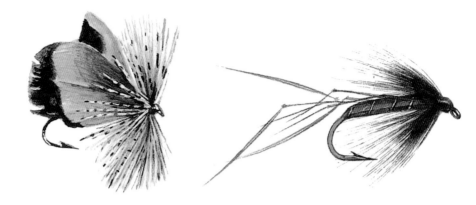

Yellow-winged Hopper

This Australian pattern is tied to imitate the yellow-winged locust (*Gastrimargus musicus*), a common species throughout Australia. There are a number of hopper patterns used in Australia; this is just one of them.

Hook	Down-eyed 8–10
Thread	Brown
Tail	Golden pheasant crest
Body	Yellow silk
Rib	Fine gold wire
Hackle	Mixed golden pheasant tippet and brown partridge
Wing	Two small black-tipped duck wing feathers dyed yellow

Red Crane Fly

This fly is a popular pattern from the west coast of Ireland. It is used on the famous Delphi fishery on the loughs Finlough, Doolough, and Glencullin, dark lakes swept by Atlantic winds and famous for sea-trout and salmon. The fly can be fished dry on the surface or just below. It is usually fished on a top dropper.

Hook	8–6
Thread	Prewaxed black or brown
Body	Red lurex or mylar
Rib	Oval gold tinsel
Hackle	Dark red cock
Wing	Two dark red cock hackle points
Legs	Knotted cock pheasant tail fibers

Cicada

The cicada comes into its own in the warmer climes of southern Europe and further south. Though there are American imitations, the most realistic I have seen comes from New Zealand. This pattern was created by Brian Hussey of Taupo, North Island. Originally from Wales, he settled as a professional guide in New Zealand in the late 1950s.

Hook	6–8
Thread	Prewaxed light green
Body	Foam plastic, colored green
Wing	Varnished cree hackles tied wonderwing-style by stroking the hackle fibers backwards then varnishing with clear cellulose or PVC
Head	Clipped white deer hair colored green

Hardy's Favorite

Like flies such as the Wickham's Fancy and the John Storey, this pattern is a fancy dry fly representing nothing in particular. However, the trout find something edible about its appearance. It has also been used as a sea-trout fly.

Hook	12–14
Thread	Black
Tail	Fibers of brown mallard feather
Body	Peacock herl
Rib	Red silk
Hackle	Dark partridge
Wing	Brown turkey

Nevamis Mayfly

This fly is John Goddard's imitation of the mayfly. It has good floating properties which were used by Goddard to great effect during the annual hatch of mayflies on the River Kennet in the U.K.

Hook	Long shank fine wire 8
Thread	Yellow
Tail	Cock pheasant tail fibers
Body	Cream seal's fur
Rib	Oval gold
Hackle	Palmered honey cock wound down the hook and clipped ¾ in. at the head down to ⅛ in. at the tail. Small furnace hackle at the head
Wing	Pale blue dun cock hackle fibers set in a "V" upright

Henry's Fork Hopper

This hopper pattern uses the buoyant properties of elk or deer hair to aid its floating potential. The fly is named after the famous Henry's Fork River, U.S.

Hook	Long shank 6–10
Thread	Prewaxed yellow
Body	Light cream-colored elk hair (reversed)
Rib	Yellow tying thread
Underwing	Yellow deer hair
Overwing	Lacquered hen pheasant body feather tied roof-style over the body
Head	Elk hair tied bullet-style with the tips flared to form a flanking collar

Fratnik's Black Sedge

This pattern was devised by Marjan Fratnik of Milan, formerly of Most Na Soci in Slovenia. The fly utilizes the cul-de-canard for the wing.

Hook	10–14
Thread	Prewaxed black
Body	Black poly dubbing
Hackle	Palmered black cock
Head hackle	Black cock (optional)
Wing	Cul-de-canard

Fratnik's Brown Sedge and Grey Sedge

Follow the pattern above but use brown poly dubbing and a brown hackle for the Brown Sedge and grey poly dubbing and either a grey or grizzle hackle.

Red Fox

Created by the New Zealand fly-tier R.K. Bragg, this is very similar in appearance to the British Blue Dun, and like its U.K. counterpart it is supposed to represent a similar natural ephemerid.

Hook	14–16
Thread	Yellow
Tail	Light natural red cock
Body	Blue squirrel fur mixed with hare's ear
Rib	Fine flat gold tinsel
Hackle	Light red cock with blue dun cock in front

John Storey

John Storey was keeper on the River Rye in Yorkshire. The fly created by him can be classed as a fancy dry fly, imitating nothing in real life except, perhaps, some form of terrestrial beetle, or even a species of Hymenoptera. Whatever it represents, it is still a popular pattern in the North of England.

Hook	12–16
Thread	Black
Body	Peacock herl
Hackle	Natural Rhode Island Red
Wing	Gray mallard tied forward of the hook

Swiss May

I picked up this pattern on a visit to Lausanne on Lake Geneva. I believe the pattern comes from the Swiss Jura.

Hook	10
Thread	Prewaxed red
Tail	Cock pheasant tail fibers
Body	Red silk
Rib	Fine oval gold
Hackle	Natural red cock
Wing	Black and white spotted guinea fowl

The Orange Stimulator

A broad-spectrum dry fly devised by the American fly-dresser Randall Kaufmann. It can be used in various sizes to imitate a stonefly, large caddis, or a hopper pattern.

Hook	Long shank 8–10
Thread	Prewaxed yellow or orange
Tail	Deer hair
Body	Dark orange antron or similar fur
Rib	Fine gold wire
Body hackle	Palmered grizzle cock hackle
Hackle	Grizzle cock tied through the thorax
Wing	Deer hair
Thorax	Bright orange antron or similar fur

Yellow Stimulator and Green Stimulator

Substitute yellow or olive, respectively, for orange in the pattern above.

Rat-faced McDougal

An excellent high-floating American fly. The deer hair body renders the fly unsinkable. In larger sizes it has often been used as a dry fly for salmon.

Hook	10–14
Thread	White
Tail	Dark ginger cock hackle fibers
Body	Clipped deer hair
Hackle	Dark ginger cock
Wing	Ginger variant (cree) hackle tips

Delta Caddis

Created by Larry Soloman, this adult caddis imitation copies a dead, or spent caddis lying exhausted in the surface film, after ovipositing. There are a number of color combinations for the Delta Caddis. Another popular variation has an olive green body and gray hackle-tip wings.

Hook	10–14
Thread	Brown
Body	Olive synthetic dubbing
Hackle	Brown cock
Wing	Brown cock hackle tips set at 45 degrees to hook shank

Taff's Black Gnat

I devised this pattern using up some modern materials from Traun River Products of Siegsdorf, Germany. The wings are made from an iridescent sheet called spectraflash which reflects all colors of the rainbow as it catches the sun. The natural fly's wing does the same. The fly is used to imitate any of the terrestrial Bibio species of gnat.

Hook	14–18
Thread	Prewaxed black
Body	Black feather herl
Hackle	Black cock
Wing	Cut and shaped from spectraflash sheet
Thorax	Thin black foam plastic (this is tied in over the hackle)

Fluttering Stonefly

A large bushy fly devised to imitate such stoneflies as *Pteronacys californica*, sometimes referred to as the Salmon Fly.

Hook	8–10
Thread	Prewaxed orange
Body	Twisted poly yarn tied as a detached projection beyond the bend of the hook
Hackle	Brown saddle
Wing	Elk hair
Antennae	Monofilament nylon dyed brown

Fluttering Golden Stonefly

Follow the pattern above but use yellow tying thread and a yellow yarn body with a light ginger cock hackle.

Low-floater Yellow Stonefly

This pattern is devised to sit lower on the water, perhaps as a spent stonefly. A small piece of fluorescent yarn is tied in at the top of the wing as a visual aid for the angler.

Hook	Long shank 8–12
Thread	Prewaxed yellow
Tail	A bunch of elk hair tied short
Body	Yellow yarn or silk
Rib	Clipped palmered brown cock hackle
Hackle	Brown cock clipped top and bottom
Wing	Light-colored elk hair with a tuft of fluorescent yellow yarn on the top
Antennae	Yellow-dyed monofilament

Low-floater Orange

Follow the pattern above but use orange yarn or silk for the body, and brown-dyed monofilament for the antennae.

Muha Reka

A Slovenian pattern developed from Marjan Fratnik's cul-de-canard "F" Fly, like the Klinkhammer fly of Hans Van Klinken, it can be described as an emerger. In this instance it can represent a hatching caddis. The translation of Muha Reka is River Fly.

Hook	Down-eyed fine wire size 12–14
Thread	Black
Body	Thinly dubbed with cul-de-canard feather fibers (optional)
Hackle	Palmered cul-de-canard
Wing	cul-de-canard

Bristol Hopper

This fly first saw the light of day on the long-established reservoirs Chew and Blagdon in the west of England. It is fished on or just below the surface and represents natural creatures such as the crane fly. It is a broad-spectrum pattern; the trout see it as a natural insect of some sort or another. The pattern can be tied in a wide range of natural colors; the olive version is depicted here.

Hook	Down-eyed 8–12
Thread	Olive
Body	Olive seal's fur or similar
Rib	Fine pearl Lurex
Hackle	Brown cock
Legs	Knotted cock pheasant tail fibers

Preska Sedge

This is another fly mentioned by Charles Ritz in his book *Fly Fisher's Life*. The fly was first tied in the late 1940s by T. Prescawiec and is one of the original truly French caddis patterns. It is still a popular pattern in France even though many more French flies imitating various species of the family Trichoptera are now available.

Hook	10–14
Thread	Prewaxed black or brown
Body	Brown condor quill (dyed-brown goose substitute)
Hackle	Brown cock
Wing	Brown mallard breast feathers tied flanking the hook

Griffith's Gnat

This is the name given to this pattern in the U.S. It was first used as a trout fly but is a universal pattern and one of the finest grayling flies I have used. I was introduced to it by Edgar Pitzenbauer of Regensberg in Bavaria, who uses this fly on many of the fine Slovenian rivers. It owes a lot to many of the early British grayling flies. In Slovenia the fly is known as the Grey Palmer.

Hook	12–18
Thread	Prewaxed brown or black
Body	Peacock herl
Hackle	Palmered grizzle cock

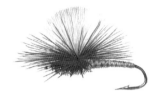

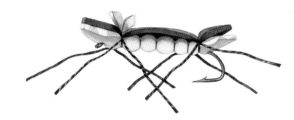

Klinkhammer

This excellent fish-catching fly was devised by the innovative Dutch fly-tier Hans Van Klinken for both trout and grayling. The fly, which hangs down in the water supported by the parachute hackle, could be classed as an "emerger," an aquatic insect on the point of hatching; whatever the classification, the trout certainly find it extremely attractive. It has been effective on English chalk streams.

Hook	Living Larva hook sizes 10–16
Thread	Black
Body	Fine medium gray fur dubbing
Hackle	Brown cock parachute style
Wing post	White polypropylene yarn

Chernobyl Ant

This fly from the U.S. has found great favor on many freestone rivers but it is in Argentina and Chile where it proved highly successful for the big fish that live in their pristine rivers. The trout perhaps take this large fly as some sort of hopper, as it is too big to be an ant. This pattern is also used as a strike indicator; a length of leader material is attached to the bend of the hook and a nymph is attached to the end. This type of fly-fishing was developed in New Zealand.

Hook	Long shank down-eyed dry fly hook size 6–12
Thread	Black, orange, or yellow
Body	Yellow closed cell foam with black foam over. (Variations include orange and black, all black, etc.)
Wing (indicator)	White foam
Legs	Rubber legs or Flexi Floss

wet flies

The trout finds most of its food beneath the surface of the water, sometimes by grubbing around the weed-beds, at other times by rising in water to take nymphs and pupae on their way to the surface.

The wet flies depicted in this section fall into various categories: larval and pupal forms of various aquatic insects; drowned adults or even swamped stillborn flies; and drowned terrestrials such as beetles. Many do not represent anything in nature, but are classed as attractor flies, designed to tempt the fish to take out of curiosity. A number of the silver-bodied flies can emulate small fry. Most of the flies given in the dry-fly section have their wet-fly equivalents. The use of heavier hooks, softer hen hackles instead of cock, and in the case of winged flies a backward-sloping wing, changes the dry fly into a wet one. Cock hackles are used for these patterns but they are taken from the very young bird where the individual fibers are very soft.

There are two main areas of wet-fly fishing. Firstly, there are the wild rain-fed rivers and streams where it is difficult to see a fish rise let alone see a minute dry fly on the surface. On such waters, wet flies are used almost exclusively upstream and down, as necessity or terrain dictates. The second main area of wet-fly fishing is on lakes, lochs, and reservoirs, where the traditional drifting-boat method enables the angler to fish a team of wet flies just below the surface. This remains one of the most effective methods of taking still-water trout and is a method insisted upon in international fly-fishing competition rules.

On wild streams I often resort to the traditional, soft-hackled wet flies. The Partridge and Orange, the Snipe and Purple, the Black Spider, a wet Coch-y-Bonddu, and many others, have all taken their fair share of trout for me.

People often ask, "When do you fish a wet fly, and when a dry?" I always fish a dry-fly pattern when I see a trout rising during a hatch of natural insects. However, when the trout refuses to succumb to a dry fly, fishing just below the surface with a wet fly can often work. When no activity is obvious, it is a case for the wet fly, pure and simple.

The soft, game-bird hackles of many wet flies have the necessary mobility in the water. They pulsate and "kick" in the current, attracting the fish by their very movement. They look alive and edible; the two key properties for a successful fly.

Cowdung

No visitor to the countryside, angler or not, can have failed to notice the hairy olive-colored flies that crawl over and buzz around freshly dropped cowpats. These terrestrial nasties are sometimes blown onto the water, where the trout show no aversion to their previous habitat. The Cowdung has been copied since the dawn of fly-dressing, and is still used by anglers of the rough streams.

Hook	12–14
Thread	Black
Body	Peacock herl
Hackle	Light natural red hen
Wing	Light brown hen quill

Grouse and Green

The Grouse series of flies is used for both trout and sea-trout. All are furnished with a wing from a grouse's tail. The Green is probably the most widely used, but the Grouse and Claret is often used as a substitute, or as an alternative to the Mallard and Claret. Others in the series include Grouse and Yellow, Grouse and Silver, Grouse and Gold, and Grouse and Blue. Only the body and hackle colors are changed.

Hook	8–16
Thread	Black or green
Tail	Golden pheasant tippet
Body	Green seal's fur
Rib	Oval gold tinsel
Hackle	Natural red or green hen
Wing	Grouse tail

Partridge and Orange

One of the classic English North Country spider-style flies, now used all over the fly-fishing world. It is an effective imitation of many of the early stoneflies (Plecoptera).

Hook	12–16
Thread	Orange
Body	Orange silk
Hackle	Brown partridge

Partridge and Yellow

A lighter version of the previous fly, this one is found with very little alteration in northern Spain and also in Italy. It is thought to imitate some of the olives.

Hook	12–16
Thread	Yellow
Body	Yellow silk
Hackle	Light partridge breast

Snipe and Purple

Though fished in many parts of the British Isles, this fly is as Yorkshire as Yorkshire pudding. Ask any fly fisherman from that county what fly he would not be without and the reply would come back—Snipe and Purple. This fly is a wet version of the iron blue (*Baetis niger* or *B. pumilus*).

Hook	12–16
Thread	Purple
Body	Purple
Hackle	A hackle from inside a snipe's wing

Butcher

This fly is a long-established attractor pattern. Its history is well documented, being the creation of two gentlemen from Tunbridge Wells in the U.K., one of whom was a butcher by trade. The colors of the fly supposedly represent the hallmarks of his trade, blood and a blue apron. This fly has continued to catch fish on still waters and rivers since the day of its invention over 150 years ago. The Gold Butcher has a gold tinsel body instead of silver.

Hook	10–14 (larger sizes for sea-trout)
Thread	Black
Tail	Red ibis substitute
Body	Flat silver tinsel
Rib	Oval silver tinsel
Hackle	Black hen
Wing	Blue mallard quill feather

Poult Bloa

The term "bloa" is from the same root as "blae," meaning a smoky bluish gray. This spider fly is used as an imitation of many of the ephemerids and is a wet version of the pale watery.

Hook	14–16
Thread	Yellow
Body	Lightly dubbed blue dun fur on yellow silk
Hackle	A hackle from the inside of a young grouse wing

Zulu

This is also a very old pattern, used for both lake and sea-trout. In larger versions it is used as a dapping fly.

Hook	8–14
Thread	Black
Tail	Red wool
Body	Black silk
Rib	Silver oval
Hackle	Palmered black cock

Soldier Palmer

A top fly used on such waters as Grafham in the U.K., the Soldier Palmer goes from strength to strength. Usually fished as the top dropper on a team of three traditional flies, this fly accounts for many fish. It is possible that this pattern is the original artificial fly. Some anglers call for a red tail on this fly, but this is optional.

Hook	8–14
Thread	Black
Tail	Red wool (optional)
Body	Red wool
Rib	Gold or silver wire
Hackle	Palmered medium red cock or hen

Mallard and Claret

This is probably the most effective of the Mallard series. It is a traditional pattern still used by today's anglers on still waters. Other flies in the series are Mallard and Yellow, Mallard and Blue, Mallard and Green, Mallard and Black, Mallard and Silver, Mallard and Orange and so on. All that alters is the body and hackle color.

Hook	8–14
Thread	Black
Tail	Golden pheasant tippet
Body	Claret seal's fur, or wool
Rib	Oval gold tinsel
Hackle	Black or claret hen
Wing	Bronze mallard shoulder

Invicta

One of the most popular fly patterns ever conceived and still a firm favorite with both still-water anglers and sea-trout fishermen. The fly was created by James Ogden of Cheltenham, thought to be the creator of the dry fly as we know it today. The Invicta is a superb pattern during a sedge fly rise, perhaps imitating a hatching caddis or a returning egg-laying female of a species that descends beneath the water surface to oviposit.

Hook	8–14
Thread	Black or yellow
Tail	Golden pheasant crest
Body	Yellow seal's fur
Rib	Gold wire or oval
Hackle	Palmered light red cock with blue jay at the throat
Wing	Hen pheasant center tail or wing, which is a little easier to use

Black Pennell

This is one of a famed series of flies devised by Victorian author Cholmondeley Pennell for both trout and sea-trout. The black version is extremely effective during a rise of chironomid midges. In larger sizes, it is considered to be a useful sea-trout fly. The other color variation still in use today is the Claret Pennell.

Hook	8–14
Thread	Black
Tail	Golden pheasant tippets
Body	Black silk
Rib	Oval silver tinsel or flat if preferred
Hackle	Black cock or hen

Coachman

This is a particular favorite of mine. With its bright white wing, the fly is particularly useful at dusk. I always fish it as a wet fly, although some anglers favor a dry version. The fly was created in the nineteenth century, supposedly by a coachman to the reigning monarch. Many people feel that it is an impression of a moth of sorts. A variant known as the Leadwing Coachman sports a more somber gray wing.

Hook	8–14
Thread	Black
Body	Peacock herl
Hackle	Natural red cock or hen
Wing	White goose

Royal Coachman

The humble Coachman fly was taken to the U.S., where its livery was livened up with a red vest. This fly is a standard wet pattern in the Americas. It has made the return journey to the U.K., where it proves quite useful as an attractor pattern in colored water on rivers and lakes.

Hook	8–14
Thread	Black
Tail	Golden pheasant tippet
Body	Bronze peacock herl with red silk center
Hackle	Natural red cock or hen
Wing	White goose

Dunkeld

A few years ago I was a guest at an international fly-fishing match. Before the match, I wandered between the teams huddled together in secret conclave. All were secretly settling on flies to be used that day and unbeknown to each other, each team had chosen the Dunkeld as one of their trio of flies. This fly of Scottish origin is a firm favorite of the reservoir angler. The original fly called for cheeks of Jungle cock, but nowadays they are usually omitted.

Hook	8–12
Thread	Black or orange
Tail	Golden pheasant crest
Body	Flat gold tinsel
Rib	Oval gold rib tinsel
Hackle	Palmered orange cock
Wing	Bronze mallard, with Jungle cock cheeks (optional)

Green Peter

This fly is fished wet or dry and represents a sedge. The origin of this pattern is firmly in the Emerald Isle where it is used to great effect on the famed lakes of that country. Like the Bibio (opposite), it is a popular pattern amongst reservoir anglers.

Hook	8–12
Thread	Black or olive
Body	Light green seal's fur (pea green)
Rib	Fine oval gold
Hackle	Palmered ginger cock, another ginger cock at the head
Wing	Hen pheasant or light brown speckled hen

Bibio

This fly is Irish in origin, but in recent years it has received wide attention throughout the British Isles. The Bibio is a group of true flies which includes the Black Gnat and the Hawthorn. Another version has a black/red/black/red body. This fly is best fished as a bob fly in the surface film.

Hook	10–14
Thread	Black
Body	Black seal's fur with a claret seal's fur center
Rib	Silver wire or oval
Hackle	Palmered black cock

Alexandra

Truly an attractor pattern, this was named after Queen Alexandra when she was a princess. It was originally called the Lady of the Lake evoking the Arthurian legends. In its early days this fly was considered too deadly and was banned on some waters. Today, though used by some die-hard lake fishermen, the Alexandra comes into its own as a sea-trout fly.

Hook	8–12
Thread	Black
Tail	Red ibis substitute and two or three peacock sword-tail fibers
Body	Flat silver tinsel
Rib	Oval silver tinsel
Hackle	Black cock or hen
Wing	Green peacock sword flanked with strips of red ibis substitute (scarlet swan)

March Brown

The natural march brown (*Rhithrogena haarupi*) is extremely local and occurs on very few rivers. Yet the artificial fly is fished in all corners of the British Isles. Most areas have their own individual patterns: the Red-legged March Brown, the Claret March Brown, even a Purple March Brown. The fly is an insect of the wild rocky rivers, not of the sedate chalk streams, although it is found in Normandy.

Hook	8–14
Thread	Black or brown
Tail	Partridge tail fibers
Body	Hare's ear and body fur mixed
Rib	Gold wire
Hackle	Brown partridge
Wing	Hen pheasant wing slips

Black Spider

This is not an imitation of a spider as such, but the word "spider" indicates the style of dressing. A sparse mobile hackle that kicks and pulsates in the water is the hallmark of the spider-dressed flies. The Black Spider is a must for all rough stream fishing anywhere in the world.

Hook	12–18
Thread	Black
Body	Black silk
Hackle	Black hen

Peter Ross

A lake and sea-trout fly of proven worth evolved by Peter Ross of Perthshire in the late nineteenth century. He altered the already-established Teal and Red and turned a good pattern into a more killing one, so that today, as far as the Teal series of flies is concerned, the Peter Ross heads the list.

Hook	8–12
Thread	Black
Tail	Golden pheasant tail fibers
Body	Two-thirds silver tinsel, one-third red seal's fur
Rib	Oval silver tinsel
Hackle	Black cock or hen
Wing	Barred teal flank

Gosling

An Irish pattern for the great limestone lakes of that country, this fly is an imitation of the mayfly and is fished wet or just in the surface film. This particular Gosling was created by Michael Rogan, Ballyshannon, in the family fly-dressing business of that name. Rogan's was famed for its exquisite salmon flies, which were all tied without the aid of a vice. In the mid-nineteenth century, Francis Francis described Rogan's fly as a "piece of jewelry."

Hook	8–10
Thread	Yellow
Tail	Cock pheasant tail fibers
Body	Golden olive seal's fur
Rib	Gold wire
Hackle	Orange cock with gray speckled mallard in front

York's Special

This fly, known as the Yorkie in North Wales fishing circles, is a popular pattern for the lakes of the Principality. It was created by a gentleman called York who traveled the area selling flies and other items of tackle to the local stores. The York's Special is a good fly to use when the heather fly (sometimes called the Bloody Doctor), which looks like a hawthorn with red legs, falls on the water.

Hook	10–14
Thread	Black
Tail	Red-dyed swan or goose
Body	Peacock herl
Hackle	Coch-y-Bonddu

Diawl Bach

As its name indicates, this is a Welsh fly. Diawl Bach translated means Little Devil. Though Welsh by birth, this pattern has achieved its greatest success on such waters as Chew Valley and Blagdon reservoirs in the U.K.

Hook	12–14
Thread	Black or brown
Tail	Brown cock hackle fibers
Body	Peacock herl
Hackle	Dark brown hen

Black and Peacock Spider

A simple, hackled wet fly that goes back to the days of early fly-tying, it was brought to light and popularized by Tom Ivens, one of the pioneers of modern reservoir fishing. Some believe that this fly represents a species of aquatic snail, although I am inclined to believe that the trout take this fly because it looks edible and can represent a wide number of small creatures, both aquatic and terrestrial. I am never without this pattern when I fish the wilder lakes or reservoirs of the U.K.

Hook	8–14
Thread	Black
Body	Peacock herl
Hackle	Black hen

Blae and Black

A traditional lake pattern originating in Ireland, but now used all over the British Isles. It is particularly effective during a rise of chironomid midges. In some places this fly is known as the Duck Fly. It can also be a useful fly for sea-trout.

Hook	8–12
Thread	Black
Tail	Golden pheasant tippets (alternatively, black cock hackle fibers)
Body	Black floss
Rib	Oval silver tinsel
Hackle	Black cock or hen
Wing	Gray duck

Picket Pin

Though this American pattern is classed as a wet fly fished on a sunk line slowly along the bottom, it has taken a number of good trout for me. It is possible that the trout mistook the fly for a dragonfly larva. It is best to weight the pattern.

Hook	Long shank 8–12
Thread	Black
Tail	Brown cock hackle fibers
Body	Bronze peacock herl
Hackle	Palmered with brown cock
Wing	Gray squirrel. A head of peacock herl is tied in after the wing

Dr. Sprately

I first came across this North American pattern in Wales of all places, where a number of my friends were taking good bags with this fly. Sometimes known as Doc Sprately, or just Sprately, this fly was named after Dr. Donald A. Sprately from Mount Vernon, Washington State and was created by Dick Prankard around 1949. This fly was one of the most popular patterns used in British Columbia, Canada.

Hook	Long shank 8–10
Thread	Black
Tail	Grey cock hackle fibers
Body	Black wool
Rib	Flat silver tinsel
Hackle	Grizzle cock
Wing	Pheasant tail fibers. A peacock herl head is tied in after the wing

Orange Woodcock

This fly hails from New Zealand, where it fills the role of such British flies as the Partridge and Orange.

Hook	10–16
Thread	Orange
Body	Orange wool
Rib	Fine silver tinsel
Hackle	Woodcock

Parmachene Belle

Probably one of the best-known American wet-fly patterns. With its striking red and white garb, it is easily recognizable by most anglers. It is an attractor fly and has a number of devotees among the British still-water brigade.

Hook	8–12
Thread	Black or yellow
Tail	Red and white cock hackle fibers
Body	Yellow floss
Rib	Flat gold tinsel
Hackle	Mixed red and white cock
Wing	White goose with center strip of red-dyed goose

Carter's Pink Lady

I brought back a number of specimens of this fly from South Africa and have used them on my local waters where they have behaved no worse than any other fly. I have since tied a few specimens with a fluorescent pink floss for sea-trout.

Hook	8–10
Thread	Black
Tail	Speckled hen fibers
Body	Pink wool
Hackle	Speckled hen

Kenya Bug

Here is a pattern that could well fall into the nymph category. As the fly's name suggests, it is used right up into Kenya.

Hook	8–12
Thread	Black
Tail	Black cock hackle fibers (alternatively, a blue guinea fowl)
Body	Black wool
Rib	Silver tinsel
Hackle	Long-fibered black hen

Taddy

An excellent South African fly that imitates the young frog. Trout in dams quite often selectively feed on these creatures. It is then that the Taddy comes into its own.

Hook	8–12
Thread	Black
Tail and body	Both made from the same bunch of black squirrel hair

Pallaretta

A traditional fly from Spain that is fished both sides of the Pyrenees. The feathers for most Spanish flies come from the fabled cocks of Leon, whose superb spade feathers have a glass-like finish. Their color is called Indio Acerado (steel gray). In many of the traditional Spanish wet flies the hackle does not go completely around the hook, only above and around the sides.

Hook	12
Thread	Black or brown
Body	Yellow silk varnished
Rib	Black silk
Hackle	Dark blue dun cock

Mave

Another Spanish fly tied in the traditional Spanish wet-fly style. This time the feather used for the hackle is called Flor de Escoba (of a color of the Flower of the Mountain Broom). All mottled feathers are prefixed by the word Prado and plain hackles are prefixed Indio. If a white hackle is used (Indio Palometa) then another traditional fly, the Albernios Pena, can be tied. The Mave could be classed as the Snipe and Purple of Spain.

Hook	12–14
Thread	Pale yellow (primrose)
Body	Purple silk
Rib	Primrose silk
Hackle	Mottled spade hackle fibers (Flor de Escoba)

Red Bartellini Spider

This pattern is one in a series, created by Walter Bartellini of Turin. They are used for trout and grayling on such rivers as the Orco, Po, and Stura. Unlike other Italian patterns they use modern materials such as fluorescent silks. In most cases, the emphasis is on the color of the head, which is often of a totally different color to the body of the fly. This color feature is similar to the flies used in the Spanish Pyrenees although not apparent in other European or American spider flies.

Hook	Grub type 16–20
Thread	Red
Body	Fluorescent red silk
Hackle	White hen
Head	Fluorescent green silk

Red Valasesiana

This type of fly comes from the Sesia Valley in the Piedmont region of northern Italy, bordering on Switzerland. These patterns have been in use on the River Sesia for over 200 years, the first reference to them appearing in church chronicles around 1760. They were originally fished using hazel or ash poles, about 11–13 feet long, with a line of braided male horsehair, a gut leader, and four flies.

Hook	10–16
Thread	Red
Body	Red silk
Hackle	Gray/blue dun cock

Black Valasesiana

This is another variation of the Valasesiana fly. These Italian flies are traditionally tied on blind (eyeless) hooks. To tie on eyed hooks, an ideal model is the Partridge "Grub" hook.

Hook	10–16
Thread	Black
Body	Black silk
Hackle	Black hen

Ossolina Nymph Style

This fly hails from the Ossola valley to the west of the Sesia valley in the Piedmont area of Italy. Both this fly and the Ossolina Emerger (right) originate from the town of Domobossala and were partially tied by machine which is unique in the world of fly dressing.

Hook	16–18
Thread	Brown
Tail	Cock pheasant tail fibers
Body	Cock pheasant tail fibers
Rib	Gold wire
Hackle	A few wisps of gray feather emerging from the head of the fly

Ossolina Emerger or Spent

This traditional Italian fly can represent an emerging aquatic insect such as a small mayfly, stonefly, or gnat. At the same time it can imitate a spent or dying insect caught in the surface film.

Hook	14–16
Thread	Black
Body	Naples yellow (dirty yellow)
Hackle	Sparse long-fibered pale ginger cock

The Silver Delphi

The fly gets its name from the famous Delphi fishery in the old kingdom of Connemara, a fishery beloved and mentioned by T. C. Kingsmill-Moore in his classic book *A Man May Fish*. The valley was given the name Delphi by the Marquis of Sligo on his return from Greece in the early nineteenth century. It was in this valley that he built his lodge, now an excellent fishing hotel. The fly is one of the best sea-trout patterns for the area.

Hook	8–14
Thread	Prewaxed black
Tail	Two small Jungle cock feathers back to back
Body	Flat silver tinsel
Rib	Silver wire
Hackle	Black cock or hen; one at the head, the other divides the body in half

Doobry

This pattern hails from the Orkneys. The fly was devised by Stan Headley and is an excellent top-dropper pattern. Most palmered flies are fished as a top dropper; the fibers of the hackle tug at the surface film in imitation of an insect's legs just as it hatches.

Hook	8–10
Thread	Prewaxed black
Tail	Fluorescent scarlet wool
Body	Flat gold tinsel
Rib	Fine oval gold tinsel
Hackles	Palmered black cock up the body, orange-dyed cock at the head

Peute

I was first told of this fly by the French angling journalist, George Lenzi. I was subsequently sent a pattern by the well-known French angler, author, and fly-dresser Raymond Rocher. The original fly was alleged to have been tied by a gypsy and the dressing given to the famous fly-dresser Bresson. The word "Peute" means ugly in one of the French dialects. The fly represents a hatching sedge of sorts.

Hook	12–18
Thread	Prewaxed yellow
Body	Formed with the tying thread
Hackle	A long-fibered wild duck feather swept back

Cuk

The Bosnian fishing writer Savo Martinovic provided me with this fly. It is tied direct to nylon and is virtually the same as those described by Skues on his visit to Bosnia in 1896 in *The Chalk Stream Angler*, 1912 by Seeley Service. The name Cuk derives from the onomatopoeic cry of a small owl whose feathers are used in the fly's construction.

Hook	10
Thread	Brown
Body	Dark green silk
Rib	Brown thread
Wing	A feather from a small brown owl

Poil de Lievre

The English translation is Hair of the Hare. The fly hails from Brittany and was created by the father of the famous French fly-dresser André Ragot whose flies are internationally known.

Hook	10–12
Thread	Prewaxed gray
Body	Hare's fur with a tip of orange silk
Hackle	Smoky-gray cock

Haul a Gwynt

This pattern from north Wales is one of the best patterns for use on some of the Welsh still waters. The translation is "sun and wind" and that is the time when it is used to best effect.

Hook	10–14
Thread	Prewaxed black
Body	Black ostrich herl
Hackle	Cock pheasant neck feather (red with black tips)
Wing	Black crow

Old Joe

This fly from the mid-Wales area is for rivers and can be considered an imitation of the dark olive. It can also be used as a dry fly if a cock and not a hen hackle is used.

Hook	12–14
Thread	Prewaxed black or brown
Tail	Cock pheasant tail fibers
Body	Cock pheasant tail
Rib	Fine gold wire
Hackle	Olive hen

Peacock Wooly Worm

The American Wooly Worm flies are popular in many fly-fishing countries. This peacock version, along with black, brown, and orange, are often used in the waters of southern Africa. All the flies are usually preweighted.

Hook	Long shank 8–12
Thread	Prewaxed black
Tail	Black cock hackle fibers and a short tuft of fluorescent scarlet wool or silk
Body	Green peacock herl
Hackle	Sparsely tied palmered black cock

Dunking Daddy

In the early fall on many still waters and reservoirs, the crane fly or daddy-longlegs, is blown onto the water surface. Struggling in the surface film, they soon come to the notice of the trout who begin feeding avidly on them. This imitation represents an unfortunate insect swamped by the water waiting to be mopped up at the trout's leisure.

Hook	Down-eyed nymph hook size 8–10
Thread	Brown
Body	Cock pheasant tail fibers or cream raffene (plastic raffia)
Underbody	Lead wire
Rib	Fine gold wire
Hackle	Brown cock
Wing	Two brown cock hackles
Legs	Knotted cock pheasant tail fibers or Flexi Floss
Head	Gold bead

Watson's Fancy

Another fancy pattern favored in Scotland and Ireland for lake fishing. Like many of the traditional loch patterns, it is also a useful sea-trout fly. The Jungle cock cheeks are now, of course, optional due to the protection of the species. However, in the U.K. birds are bred and reared solely for their feathers, which are plucked without harm to the birds, so once more many of the "Jungle cock" flies can be seen in their full glory.

Hook	8–10
Thread	Black
Tail	Golden pheasant crest
Body	Two halves red seal's fur followed by black seal's fur
Rib	Oval silver tinsel
Hackle	Black hen
Wing	Black-dyed goose or natural crow,

nymphs and pupae

At one time the term "nymph" was used to describe only the larval stage of the Ephemeroptera (the mayflies) and the Odanata (damsel and dragonflies). The larval stage of the other aquatic insects had their own generic terms.

Now, though, the term "nymph" is far broader in meaning, and has come to describe and include those flies that have been specifically designed to imitate any creature that lives below the water. Larval and pupal stages, and even adults of some creatures, are embraced by the term 'nymph', as are freshwater shrimps and the lowly water-louse, water-boatmen, and corixae, the voracious larvae of the water beetles, and the wide range of larvae and pupae of many of the aquatic true flies (Diptera). Fishing such artificials is termed "nymph-fishing." It is difficult to differentiate between fishing the nymph and fishing the wet fly as some wet flies are nymphs in concept, though not in design. Other wet flies can look very much like nymphs, and certainly some nymphs could well be described as wet flies.

Nymph-fishing started in the latter half of the nineteenth century with G. E. M. Skues. Most anglers confined their sport to casting a fly to a rising fish. When rises were not apparent on the surface, they did not fish; such was their angling Puritanism. Skues, on the other hand, contended

that the trout fed avidly below the surface on the hatching nymph and were sometimes content to do this rather than rise to the floating adult fly. Upstream wet-fly fishing as practiced by northern anglers bore witness to this. Skues adapted these wet-fly tactics to the chalk streams and developed his nymph flies to suit the water. The story goes that he was fishing a badly tied dry fly which sunk straight away. As soon as it went below the surface the fly was taken by a trout. The trout continued to take the sunken fly, ignoring any floating pattern.

Today the importance of the nymph is known by most anglers and the great influx of still-water anglers to the fishing scene has possibly made nymph fishing the prime method of taking fish.

The nymph patterns of this section are for both river and still water, and show a great variety in size and in the materials used to create them. They cover most aquatic creatures and even include some nymphs from the realms of fancy which imitate nothing in particular and yet are proven fish-takers.

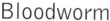

Bloodworm

This fly imitates the larval stage in the life-cycle of the chironomid midge. This creature lives buried deep in the mud and, although with its hemoglobin it can retain oxygen in its system, from time to time it must rise in order to replenish its supply of oxygen. It is at this point that it comes to the attention of the trout. The red marabou is tied not just as a tail, but also as an extension of the body, in order to give a wriggling motion to the fly.

Hook	Long shank 12–14
Thread	Red
Tail	Tuft of red marabou
Body	Red floss silk tied with distinct undulations
Rib	Fluorescent red floss
Head	Bronze peacock herl

Buzzer Pupa

This is the most important stage in the life-cycle of the midge, as far as the trout is concerned. There are many color variations of this fly, including olive, red, orange, bright green, and brown. The one depicted here is the black. The chironomid midge is perhaps the major item in the still-water trout's diet.

Hook	10–16
Thread	Black
Tail	Tuft of white fluorescent floss
Body	Black floss silk
Rib	Silver wire
Thorax	Bronze peacock herl
Breathing filaments	Tuft of white fluorescent floss or white feather fiber

Buoyant Buzzer (Suspender Buzzer)

Just prior to hatching, the pupa hangs motionless in the surface film before adopting a horizontal position for the hatching. This style of fly was devised originally by the American fly-rodder and fly-tier Charles E. Brooks, and was further developed by John Goddard the British angling entomologist.

Hook	10–16
Thread	Black
Tail	White DFM silk or wool
Body	Black seal's fur or silk
Rib	Silver wire
Wing cases	Orange goose feather slips
Thorax	Peacock herl
Head	Bead of pastazote or polystyrene wrapped in nylon mesh

Silver Corixa

This small water bug swims swiftly up to the surface in order to trap air on the underside of its abdomen. This bubble of air is then taken back down under the water. The air appears like a coating of silver beneath the insect.

Hook	12–14
Thread	Black
Body	Flat silver tinsel
Rib	Oval silver tinsel
Wing case (back)	Cock pheasant tail fibers
Paddles	Two cock pheasant tail fibers

Damsel Nymph

This is another creation of the late
Richard Walker. There are many damselfly
imitations; this one is a fair representation
and a proven killer. The Damsel Nymph is
a very good fly to use during the summer
months on any of the smaller still-water
fisheries. As soon as you see the slim blue
damsels on the wing, you will know it is
time to fish the Damsel Nymph.

Hook	Long shank 8
Thread	Olive or brown
Tail	Cock pheasant tail fibres dyed olive green
Body	Weighted first with lead strip. Mixed cobalt blue and orange lamb's wool. Synthetic dubbing can be used
Rib	Brown silk
Hackle	Grey partridge hackle dyed grass green

Dragonfly Nymph

I tied this fly up a number of years ago
and it still continues to catch fish. The
beauty of this fly is its simplicity of
construction. It is fished in the same way
as the Damsel Nymph—very slowly with
occasional spurts.

Hook	Long shank 8
Thread	Black or brown
Tail	Three short brown or olive goose biots
Body	Mixed dark brown/olive wool
Rib	Fluorescent green silk
Hackle	Brown partridge
Head	Peacock herl

Walker's Mayfly Nymph

One of the best patterns created by Richard Walker in the last few years before his untimely death, this fly is extremely popular on many of the clear still-water fisheries such as Avington in Hampshire, U.K.

Hook	Long shank 8
Thread	Brown
Tail	Four or five strands of cock pheasant tail fiber
Body	Underbody lead foil. Creamy yellow angora wool
Rib	Brown silk
Wing case	Cock pheasant tail fibers
Thorax	Same as body
Legs	Fine ends of the cock pheasant tail fibers used for wing case

Alder Larva

Brian Clarke described the alder larva as the Genghis Khan of still water. It is a voracious predator but during the months of late March and April the larva feels the pupating urge. It then leaves the sanctuary of the detritus and migrates to the bank of the river or lake in order to dig a small chamber in which to pupate. During this migration to the bankside it is preyed upon by the trout. This particular fly pattern was devised by C.F. Walker.

Hook	Long shank 10–12
Thread	Brown or black
Tail	Honey cock hackle tip
Body	Mixed brown and ginger seal's fur or substitute
Rib	Oval gold tinsel
Hackle	Honey hen palmered; head hackle brown partridge
Thorax	Hare's ear

Cove's Pheasant Tail

This fly was created by the renowned nymph fisherman Arthur Cove, one of Britain's leading still-water anglers, specifically for fishing from the banks of the large reservoirs. It is fished on a long leader and with a slow retrieve. It can represent a wide range of subaquatic pupae.

Hook	8–14
Thread	Black or brown
Body	Cock pheasant tail fibers
Rib	Silver oval, gold, or copper wire
Wing case	Cock pheasant tail fibers
Thorax	Rabbit fur

Sawyer's Pheasant Tail

One of the classic flies of the chalk stream, devised by the late Frank Sawyer, the world-renowned "Keeper of the Stream." He looked after his stretch of the River Avon in Hampshire, U.K., for many years and became an acknowledged authority on the ways of the trout. His flies were created for the induced-take method of fishing.

Hook	12–16
Thread	Brown
Tail	Cock pheasant tail fibers
Body	Cock pheasant tail fibers wound with copper wire
Wing case	Cock pheasant tail fibers
Thorax	A ball of copper wire covered with cock pheasant tail fibers

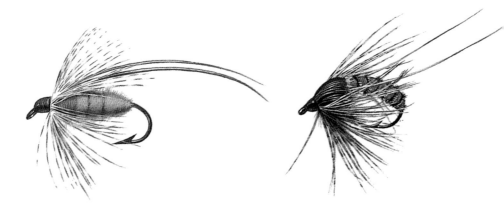

Green Longhorn

This fly is one of many sedge pupae patterns. The actual sedge/caddis pupa is a quiescent creature, lying in its shelter while changing into an adult in much the same way as a caterpillar rests in a chrysalis. The correct term for such flies is hatching sedge or caddis, rather than sedge pupa. There are a number of different body colors for this fly: green, orange/amber, cream, and brown.

Hook	10–12
Thread	Yellow
Body	Sea-green dyed lamb's wool on rear two-thirds; one-third sepia lamb's wool
Rib	Fine gold oval over green part of body only
Hackle	Brown partridge
Horns	Two cock pheasant tail fibers

Swannundaze Sedge Pupa

Here I have used a modern plastic strip called "Swannundaze" introduced to fly-dressers by Frank Johnson of New Jersey, U.S. By using a fluorescent underbody of red silk with the amber Swannundaze over it, one gets a blood-like effect in the abdomen of the fly. I first published this pattern in *Trout Fisherman*, January 1982.

Hook	Shrimp hook size 8–10
Thread	Yellow
Body	Underbody fluorescent red silk; overbody clear amber Swannundaze
Rib	Strand of peacock herl between Swannundaze turns
Hackle	Brown partridge
Wing case	Cock pheasant tail fibers
Thorax	Brown seal's fur or substitute
Horns	Cock pheasant tail fibers

Gray Goose

The second of Frank Sawyer's quartet of river nymphs, this pattern is used instead of the Pheasant Tail when a lighter pattern is required. Frank Sawyer did not choose the materials for his flies because they imitated natural nymph colors, but because the trout found them attractive.

Hook	12–14
Thread	Gray or white
Tail	Gray goose fibers
Body	Gray goose
Rib	None, but copper wire is wound with the goose fibers
Thorax	Gray goose fibers

Shrimper

The freshwater shrimp (*Gammarus pulex*) is an important item in the diet of the trout, in both rivers and still waters. There are many "shrimp" flies. This one is sold commercially by a number of fly-dressing houses.

Hook	10–14
Thread	Brown or olive
Body	Olive seal's fur weighted with lead
Rib	Orange silk
Hackle	Palmered olive cock
Back	Clear polythene

Golden Shrimp

Freshwater shrimps come in a wide range of colors such as gray and olive. Some have a distinct orange glow. Often during molting, and certainly when dead, they are yellow. Yellow seems to be a good color to use when the water is muddy and the fish take it well in these conditions.

Hook	Shrimp hook 8–10
Thread	Yellow
Body	Golden yellow seal's fur
Rib	Lead wire
Hackle	Golden yellow cock
Back	Yellow raffene or latex
Feelers	Yellow cock hackle fibers

Iron Blue Nymph

A river nymph designed to imitate the natural iron blue nymph stage, *Baetis pumilis* or *B. niger*, this fly hatches out in very large numbers on many rivers in the U.K.

Hook	14–16
Thread	Black or claret
Tail	Iron blue cock hackle fibers
Body	Mole fur
Rib	Fine silver wire
Wing case	Black feather fiber
Thorax	Mole fur

Pond Olive Nymph

This simple nymph imitates the larval stage of the ephemerid *Cloeon dipterum*. This tiny fly can hatch out in very large numbers on some British still waters.

Hook	14
Thread	Olive
Tail	Olive cock hackle fibers
Body	Dark olive seal's fur or synthetic substitute
Rib	Fine gold wire
Wing case	Pale olive goose or swan fiber
Thorax	Dark olive seal or substitute

Orange Nymph

I devised this pattern to imitate (albeit very much larger) a form of Daphnia. Trout often become preoccupied with feeding on these minute creatures, swallowing them down in their hundreds, and the Orange Nymph has proved successful on such occasions. It is impossible to imitate the exact size of the Daphnia, because they are far too small.

Hook	14–16
Thread	Orange
Body	Orange seal's fur
Rib	Gold wire (optional)
Wing case (back)	Orange swan or goose feather tied across the back
Feelers	Two strands of goose left unclipped

Montana Nymph

What a good fly this pattern is; big, black, and bold, it was originally tied to represent the creeper (larva) of the black willow stonefly. As its name indicates, it hails from the state of Montana, U.S., where it is used on the Yellowstone and Missouri rivers. In the U.K. it has proved a good fly for reservoir use.

Hook	Large shank 6–10
Thread	Black
Tail	Two black cock hackle tips
Body	Black chenille
Hackle	Black cock wound through the thorax
Wing case	Black chenille
Thorax	Yellow chenille

Cockwill's Lead Nymph

Peter Cockwill has caught so many large fish in his career that it does not bear thinking about. This particular simple nymph is used only on clear waters where you can see your fish. The fly is cast in the fish's path, allowed to sink, then raised to induce the take.

Hook	8–10
Thread	Black or olive
Tail	Olive floss
Body	Close turns of lead wire
Hackle/legs	Olive floss
Wing case	Olive floss
Thorax	Olive floss

Long-tail Damsel

When disturbed the natural damsel nymph swims with a very swift, undulating body movement. This fly of Peter Cockwill's is tied to emulate the natural creature's movement. It is usually fished on a slow sink line and with an exceptionally fast retrieve.

Hook	Long shank 8–10 or standard size 6–8 (weighted)
Thread	Black or olive
Tail	Olive marabou
Body	Black and olive chenille
Hackle	Palmered olive cock

Swannundaze Stonefly Creeper

This fly was devised by Frank Johnson of Lyndhurst, New Jersey, using the versatile Swannundaze nymph body material which he markets throughout the world. The fly was tested on the Beaverkill and Delaware rivers and was not found wanting.

Hook	Long shank 12–16
Thread	Black or brown
Tail	Brown goose biots
Underbody	Built up with two strips of heavy nylon then covered with amber fur
Overbody	Translucent brown Swannundaze nymph material
Rib	Dark brown thread
Wing case	Cock pheasant church window feathers
Thorax	Amber fur
Legs	Brown partridge
Antennae	Goose biots

Blue-winged Olive Nymph

This nymph, as its name suggests, imitates the larval form of the blue-winged olive in the U.S., such species as *Ephemerella cornuta* and others, as well as the British species *E. ignita.*

Hook	14–18
Thread	Olive
Tail	Wood duck fibers
Body	Medium olive fur
Rib	Brown silk
Hackle	Brown partridge feathers
Wing case	Gray goose wing fibers
Thorax	Medium olive fur

American Gold-ribbed Hare's Ear Nymph

The American version of the British G.R.H.E. with the addition of a black feather wing case, this fly catches fish on both sides of the Atlantic.

Hook	10–14
Thread	Black or brown
Tail	Hare body fur
Body	Hare fur
Rib	Gold wire
Hackle	Hare fur fibers picked out
Wing case	Black feather fiber
Thorax	Hare fur

Light Cahill Nymph

A standard American nymph pattern tied to represent the larval form of many of the indigenous mayflies in the rivers of the eastern United States.

Hook	10–18
Thread	Cream
Tail	Wood duck fibers
Body	Creamy tan fur
Hackle	Few fibers of wood duck
Wing case	Wood duck fibers
Thorax	Creamy tan fur

Dark Hendrikson Nymph

Another standard American nymph pattern devised to imitate a number of different species.

Hook	10–14
Thread	Olive
Tail	Wood duck fibers
Body	Gray brown fur
Rib	Brown silk
Hackle	Brown partridge fibers
Wing case	Turkey tail fibers
Thorax	Gray brown fur

Zug Bug

This fly appears in most lists from American fly suppliers. One of the original names for this fly was Kemp's Bug. The pattern is classed as a fancy nymph pattern.

Hook	10–14
Thread	Black
Tail	Peacock sword fibers
Body	Bronze peacock herl
Rib	Flat silver tinsel
Hackle	Brown hen, sparse
Wing case	Wood duck tied at the head (sometimes barred teal is used)

Prince

This fly, like the Zug Bug, is another popular American broad-spectrum nymph. It is reputed to have been devised by Don and Dick Olson of Minnesota and was made popular in the Western States by Dick Prince of California from whom it gets its name. It is considered to be one of the best broad spectrum nymphs in use in the U.S.A. today.

Hook	8–12
Thread	Black
Tail	Brown goose biot (sometimes black goose biot as alternative)
Body	Peacock herl
Rib	Flat gold tinsel
Hackle	Collar hackle sparse brown hen (or black)
Horns	Two slips of white swan or goose

Hare Caddis

This pattern is based on a fly tied by Darrel Martin of Tacoma, Washington State, U.S. It represents a caddis larva in its case. The dubbed fur body gives plenty of movement to the fly.

Hook	Shrimp hook or caddis or Mustad 37160 8–12
Thread	Black
Body	Dubbed hare fur
Hackle	Sparse brown partridge
Thorax	Yellow floss
Head	Black poly fur with burnt nylon for eyes

Whitlock Stonefly Creeper

Dave Whitlock is, without doubt, America's leading fly-dressing innovator and angling artist. His patterns are admired all over the fly-fishing world. He is quick to adapt both traditional and up-to-the-minute materials. His flies have influenced fly-tiers throughout the U.S. and Europe.

Hook	Long shank 2–8
Thread	Orange
Tail and antennae	Boar hair
Body	Mixed amber and orange synthetic dubbing
Rib	Copper or gold wire
Back, wing cases and back of head	Brown raffene (Swiss straw)
Legs	Church window pheasant feather dyed light gold

Teeny Nymph

A simple nymph from the west coast of the U.S., that has developed almost into a cult fly. The fly was first tied and named after Jim Teeny of Portland. It is used for all species of trout and also for steelhead.

Hook	Long shank 8–12 (also on short shank)
Thread	Black or brown
Body	Cock pheasant tail fibers
Legs	Two tufts of cock pheasant fiber points

Casual Dress

What a nice, shaggy nymph this is, with plenty of action in the water. The Casual Dress was created by one of America's leading fly-dressers Polly Rosborough. It works well as a dragonfly larva imitation.

Hook	Long shank 6–12
Thread	Black
Tail	Muskrat guard hairs and underfur
Body	Muskrat dubbing (can be weighted)
Hackle	Collar of muskrat guard hair
Head	Black ostrich herl

Martin's Monster

A large American nymph tied to imitate the nymph of a dragonfly. The body is woven from two shades of chenille. Darrel Martin, its creator, uses strips of soft leather as an underbody to create the real insect shape.

Hook	Long shank 6–8 (this can have a bend put in the shank if desired)
Thread	Brown
Body	Woven chenille, contrasting olives (other color combinations if desired)
Legs	Two bunches of knotted cock pheasant tail fibers
Head	Dubbed turkey feather flue
Eyes	Bead chain sprayed black

Half Back

This is a simple nymph of the broad spectrum variety. It imitates nothing in particular, yet has an appeal to the trout as it looks like food.

Hook	8–12
Thread	Olive or black
Tail	Brown hackle fibers
Body	Peacock herl (thorax also peacock herl)
Rib	Gold wire
Hackle	Brown cock hackle fibers
Wing	Small bunch of brown partridge hackle fibers

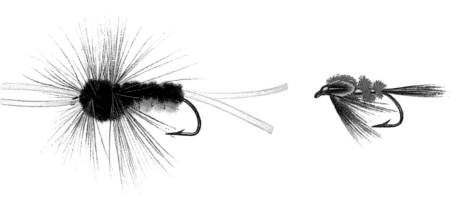

Bitch Creek Nymph

This pattern is a noted big-fish pattern for both trout and Arctic grayling. It is often preweighted with lead wire in order to fish it down on the bottom.

Hook	Long shank 6–8
Thread	Black
Tail	Two strands of white rubber
Body	Black chenille with a strand of orange chenille under secured by the tying thread. Alternatively, the body can be woven
Hackle	Three or four turns of brown cock palmered through the thorax
Thorax	Black chenille
Feelers	Two strands of white rubber

Walker's Nymph

This South African pattern was created by Lionel Walker of Walker's Killer fame (see page 146). This nymph can come in a variety of colors: green, red, and yellow. The first time I tried one of these nymphs, on a local lake, I took a 4 lb. fighting Rainbow on the very first cast.

Hook	8–12
Thread	Red
Tail	Black cock hackle fibers
Body	Red chenille
Rib	Flat gold tinsel
Hackle	Black cock
Wing case	Two brown partridge hackles flanking the body to envelop half of it

Hair Fiber Nymph

An Australian nymph with a very traditional appearance, it would serve well as a nymph for the March Brown.

Hook	10–14
Thread	Brown
Tail	Partridge tail fibers
Body	Lightly dubbed blue rabbit underfur
Rib	Oval silver tinsel
Wing case	Partridge tail
Thorax	Hare fur picked out at the sides to resemble legs

Hare and Copper Nymph

I have used this fly on both rivers and still waters in this country. It can best be described as a New Zealand version of the old favorite, the Gold-ribbed Hare's Ear. It is best fished on a floating line with a long leader.

Hook	10–14
Thread	Brown or orange
Tail	Hare fur guard hairs
Body	Hare fur (weighted)
Rib	Copper wire
Wing	Hare fur picked out

Horn Caddis

This is a New Zealand pattern that represents the caddis larva complete with a case, which can be used anywhere in the world. Fish the fly close to the bottom for the best results.

Hook	10–14
Thread	Black
Body	Gray wool tied around the bend (lacquered after the rib)
Rib	Silver wire
Hackle	Sparse grizzle cock to resemble the legs. Narrow band of white wool to resemble the body emerging from the case

NZ Orange Nymph

This nymph is tied to represent the New Zealand species of mayfly *Zephlebia cruentata* called the pepper-winged olive.

Hook	12–14
Thread	Brown or orange
Tail	Short brown partridge fibers
Body	Orange wool
Rib	Fine silver wire
Wing case	Brown partridge

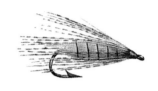

Precieuse

A French nymph from the Guy Plas
stable representing a wide range of
ephemerid nymphs. This pattern comes
in a variety of subtle body and hackle
color combinations, and is suitable for all
types of water.

Hook	12–18
Thread	Gray or black
Tail	Ash gray cock hackle fibers
Body	Light gray poly dubbing
Rib	Silver tinsel
Hackle	Short ash gray cock hackle fibers
Thorax	Dark gray

Phryga Nymph

A Guy Plas nymph imitating a hatching
sedge/caddis fly. Like the Precieuse, it can
have a number of different colored bodies.

Hook	8–10 (short shank or long shank)
Thread	Yellow
Body	Yellow and light brown mixed dubbing, tapered toward the head
Rib	Brown silk
Hackle	Ash gray cock hackle fibers, short at the top of the head
Side emergent wings	Mottled brown and gray spade cock hackle fibers

Hydropsyche

The Hydropsyche species of caddis does not make portable shelters for itself, unlike many other caddis larvae. Along with Rhyacophila species, they make webs; net-like ones in the case of Hydropsyche, purse-like in the case of Rhyacophila. Both are voracious predators and both could be imitated by this pattern of Roman Moser's.

Hook	Long shank 10
Thread	Black or brown
Tail	Soft, fluffy feathers from the base of a partridge hackle
Body	Body gill material
Rib	Copper wire
Hackle	Sparse partridge. Latex marked with a dark brown marker pen
Head	Squirrel fur dubbing

Grannom Pupa

This Spanish pupa pattern imitates the pupa of the early hatching sedge, the grannom, once called the greentail (*Brachycentrus subnubilis*). The grannom makes its appearance early in the fishing season. This imitation can also be used to imitate a number of other species and can be fished on still waters as well as rivers.

Hook	12
Thread	Black or brown
Body	Light brown poly dubbing
Rib	Dark brown thread
Hackle	Short tuft of brown partridge
Wing	Dark gray duck slips
Head	Reddish brown poly dubbing

Ucero

One of the leading angling authorities on the caddis fly in the U.S. is Gary Lafontaine. His book *Caddis Flies* is considered by many to be the definitive work on the subject. This hatching sedge pattern from Luis Antunez of Madrid is based on Lafontaine's patterns.

Hook	10–12
Thread	Red
Tail	Short tuft of polypropylene yarn
Body	Light brown or cinnamon polypropylene dubbing
Rib	Brown thread
Hackle	Poly yarn flared out, sloping backward

Arthofer Nymph

A popular Austrian nymph created by Louis Arthofer and used in many parts of Europe, it is fished on both rivers and still waters.

Hook	8–12
Thread	Black or brown
Tail	Three fine strands of ostrich herl dyed brown
Body	Brown ostrich herl
Hackle	Guinea fowl or partridge, clipped short
Wing case	Hen pheasant wing feather
Thorax	Copper wire

Floating Pupa

This tiny fly from Luis Antunez can imitate a wide variety of nondescript creatures found in the surface film, including the hatching micro sedges and members of the family Diptera.

Hook	16–18
Thread	Green
Body	Bright green poly dubbing or seal's fur
Rib	Brown thread

Swimming May Nymph

Almost 30 years ago Alan Bramley from Partridge's of Redditch designed the hook used in this pattern with my help. Today other hooks of a similar shape are widely available. This pattern to imitate the nymph of the *Ephemera danica* also works as an imitation of American mayfly species such as the Hexagenia.

Hook	Swimming nymph 8–12
Thread	Brown
Tail	Three cock pheasant tail fibers
Body	Cream Haretron or similar dubbing
Rib	Brown thread
Wing case	Cock pheasant tail fibers
Thorax	As body
Breathers	Very short tuft of brown marabou
Legs	Brown partridge hackle
Head	Light brown dubbing
Eyes	Burnt monofilament

Cocchetto Nymph

In the area around Milan people used to collect the silken cocoons of a species of indigenous moth. This primitive raw silk was used to form the body dubbing of nymphs; the underlying body color would show through the silk when the nymph was wet. According to Luciano Maragni of Milan, this type of fly was banned on some Slovenian rivers as it proved too killing for grayling.

Hook	14–16
Thread	Purple
Body	Moth cocoon dubbing over underbody of tying thread
Rib	Clipped palmered dark natural red cock hackle

The Dormouse Nymph

In the fruit-growing areas of Yugoslavia, one of the biggest pests and threats to the crops is the dormouse. About 200,000 have to be trapped each year and some people eat these little mice (shades of ancient Roman cuisine). The skins have no commercial value and are disposed of—except the few that find themselves in the hands of fly-dressers. This nymph devised by Marjan Fratnik uses fur from the dormouse tail. This fur almost breathes in the water when wet.

Hook	10–14 (can be weighted with lead wire)
Thread	Black
Tail	Dormouse tail fibers
Body	Fur from a dormouse tail
Wing case	Any dark feather
Thorax	Dormouse tail fur

Ephemera Swimming Nymph

This fly is a Japanese version of the Swimming May Nymph on page 114, probably tied to imitate the natural Japanese species *Ephemera japonica*. It was created by the talented author, photographer, and fly-tier Nori Tashiro of Yokohama.

Hook	Swimming nymph 8–14
Thread	Tan
Tail	Three strands of fine ostrich herl tips
Body	Dirty yellow synthetic fur
Rib	Fine oval gold tinsel
Wing case	Dark brown goose or turkey
Thorax	As body
Breathers	Natural ostrich herl
Legs	Gray partridge dyed yellow

Lucky Nymph

This pattern comes from the Baltic State of Lithuania and was tied by one of their leading fly-tiers Jonas Mikstas of Vilnius. I had the pleasure of fishing with him on a number of Lithuanian rivers and streams in August 1994. This pattern is used for trout and also grayling.

Hook	Down-eyed 10–14
Thread	Black
Tail	Gray cock hackle fibers
Body	Yellow silk
Rib	A black cock hackle palmered and clipped short
Wing case	Partridge hackle well lacquered
Thorax	As body but not pronounced
Legs	Dark gray cock hackle fibers

Peeping Caddis

Oliver Edwards is one of Britain's leading fly-tiers; his work is always in great demand and he has demonstrated his skills at fly fairs and seminars all over Europe and in the U.S.

Hook	Long shank 8–14
Thread	Brown
Body	Hare's fur well picked out to represent the case
Rib	Gold wire
Exposed body	Light colored wool
Legs	Brown partridge hackle
Head	The end of the wool body, burnt to form a little black blob
Weight	A gold bead or a split shot can be added to the end of the fly

V. R. Trout Nymph

In Lithuania our guide was fly fisherman and tier Vytautas Radaitis of Vilnius. Like Jonas Mikstas, though starved of good supplies of materials, he turns out some excellent flies.

Hook	Long shank 8–12
Thread	Black
Tail	French partridge hackle fibers
Body	Dark brown wool
Rib	Copper wire
Wing case	Striped partridge hackle
Thorax	Brown wool
Legs	Brown partridge

Bossbob's Hellgrammite

Kupica Nymph

This pattern was devised by the Chicago tyer Bob Long Jr. It is a big fly for big fish. The hellgrammite is one of the largest nymphs that trout will feed on.

Hook	Long shank 4–6, hook bent upwards
Thread	Black
Tail	A few fibers of brown filoplume and two rubber hackles
Underbody	Nymph form prepared body
Body	Peacock herl, palmered with a black hackle which is then clipped
Rib	Gold wire
Wing case	Brown feather fiber, lacquered
Breathers	Short tufts of filoplumes either side
Thorax	Peacock herl, palmered with an unclipped black hackle
Back	Brown feather fibers, heavily lacquered
Legs	Black rubber hackle
Antennae	Black rubber hackles

The Kupica River is a small feeder stream of the much larger Kupa River, which acts as the border between Slovenia and Croatia. This small fly has been tied by Mladen Merkas Goranin for trout and grayling, and is just one of a series using different-colored thorax dubbing and hackles—the brown one is depicted here. Combinations include black with black thorax, tail, and hackle; or white, brown, olive, claret, and orange; one uses a copper-wire thorax and another a Hare's Ear.

Hook	Down-eyed 12–22
Thread	Dark brown
Tail	Brown hackle fibers
Body	Stripped peacock herl
Wing	Jay wing quill section
Thorax	Brown fur dubbing
Legs	Sparse brown hen

Dark Stone

There are numerous patterns tied to imitate the larvae of the world's many stoneflies—this pattern was tied by Milos Zeman of the Czech Republic. He also ties a lighter version.

Hook	Long shank 8–12
Thread	Black
Tail	Two dark olive goose biots
Body	Black fur dubbing
Rib	Dark gray Swannundaze or Larva Lace
Wing case	Light mottled turkey
Thorax	Medium gray dubbing
Back	Dark turkey, folded and layered in three folds
Legs	Black hen hackle

Floating Dragon

This deer-hair pattern was created by the innovative fly-tier and author Randall Kaufmann. This pattern can either be fished on the surface or with a short leader and a sinking line. The buoyant nature of the deer tends to keep the fly off the bottom, and on retrieve it will dive down in a very realistic manner.

Hook	Long shank 4–8
Thread	Olive or brown
Tail	Olive or brown grizzle marabou
Body	Spun olive or brown deer hair, clipped flat underneath and a stripe across back using a waterproof pen
Wing case	Olive or brown turkey, lacquered and cut into a "V"
Legs	Two small bunches of olive or brown grizzle marabou either side of the body
Head	Olive or brown antron or fur dubbing
Eyes	Burnt monofilament

San Juan Worm

This simple fly is an imitation of a small aquatic annelid worm which if found in sufficient quantities can become an important item in the trout's diet. Due to its size and color, this pattern also makes a good copy of the larval stage of a chironomid midge, usually called the bloodworm. This very basic pattern was the creation of Gary Borger and relies on the shape of the hook to give the fly its wriggling movement on its descent through the water.

Hook	Old English bait hook 6–10
Thread	To match the body color
Body	Fluorescent red, orange, or pink yarn
Rib	Copper wire for the red body, silver for the other colors

Catfish Shrimp

The use of fish skin in the creations of fly patterns is not exactly new (see, for example, the Eel Skin Shrimp on page 126). Here the skin of the Danubian catfish is used for the back of this shrimp pattern. It was tied by Hans Nischkauer, an excellent fly-tier from Austria.

Hook	Down-eyed 10–16
Thread	Gray
Body	A dubbing wick made of silver wire and hare's ear
Underbody	Lead wire
Back	Catfish skin treated with picric acid creating a dark olive color. Dampen the skin before tying in and carry over the eye of the hook to form the head
Feelers	Brown partridge hackle fibers

Red-eyed Damsel

A great deal of fishing in South Africa is done on still waters which they call dams. The damsel- and dragon-fly imitations figure highly in the fly-boxes of the South African fly fisherman, and this pattern was created by Hugh Huntley. I had the great pleasure of driving with him from Pietermaritzburg to fish in the Drakensberg.

Hook	Long shank 8–12
Thread	Brown
Tail	Brown marabou plus two strands of crystal hair
Body	Dubbed brown marabou with crystal hair down the sides
Thorax	Brown marabou
Head	As thorax
Eyes	Red chenille

Olive Damsel

Bob Carnill is one of Britain's finest fly-tiers; his work has graced the pages of the magazine *Trout Fisherman* for more years than I can remember.

Hook	Long shank 12–14
Thread	Green
Tail	Three olive cock hackle points
Body	Olive swan or goose herl
Rib	Fine oval gold tinsel
Wing case	Olive feather fiber
Thorax	Olive fur dubbing
Legs	Olive-dyed partridge
Eyes	Olive-colored beads with black pupils

Red Spot Shrimp

Neil Patterson has many interesting flies credited to him including the "Funnel Dun" series of dry flies. This shrimp pattern is one of the most effective used on both rivers and still water. The red spot imitates those shrimps parasitized by a small Echinorhynchus round worm.

Hook	Sedge-type or grub-type hook, 8–16
Thread	Olive
Body	Olive seal's fur and mohair with a center spot of fluorescent red wool
Underbody	Lead wire
Rib	Gold wire
Back	Clear plastic over body and rib
Legs	The fur well picked out

Gold-head Hare's Ear

Many well-established patterns have been given a gold, and in some cases a silver, bead as an adornment. Pheasant Tails, Hare's Ears, Corixa, Stoneflies, and even Mayfly nymphs have been adorned. Gold-head type flies have been in use in Europe for many years—I have some Italian flies with glass beads which must go back almost 80 years, so bead-head flies are not new and on some European waters fish will shy away from such flies as they have come to know them too well.

Hook	Down-eyed 8–16
Thread	Black or brown
Tail	Guard hairs from the hare's mask
Body	Hare's ear dubbing
Rib	Oval or flat gold or pearly tinsel
Head	Gold bead

Plecionka

Poland, like many other eastern European countries, has a very fine fly-tying tradition. In the bad old days of the Cold War, we in the West were comparatively ignorant of what was going on in fly-fishing in these countries. When Polish fly fishermen came out of the cold, they surprised many with their fly-tying skills and also their prowess at nymph fishing. This pattern was sent to me by Adam Skrechota and represents a free-swimming caddis, a pupa, or even a Gammarus shrimp.

Hook	Grub hook 10–14
Thread	Brown
Body	Woven tan and lime-green yarn
Wing case	Slightly darker yarn back

Carnill's Corixa

This pattern was created by Bob Carnill. The corixa is a major food item for the trout, especially in lakes and reservoirs. There are patterns to imitate this creature in most fly-fishing countries, but this is probably one of the most realistic.

Hook	Short shank 10–12
Thread	Unwaxed white
Underbody	White wool over lead if weight needed
Belly	Silver glitter in liquid form
Back	White plastic, cut to a fingernail shape and colored with waterproof pen. Superglue to the body and pour liquid glitter to fill the underneath of the shell back. Allow to dry for 24 hours
Paddles	Two hackle stalks with a small amount of feather fiber at the tip

Polifeitus

This nymphal pattern is used for both trout and grayling and was first tied by Branko Gasparin of Nova Gorica. Unlike many of the bead-headed flies from Europe, the bead used here for the body is not slipped onto the shank but is tied on top of the hook by means of a pin. The weighted bead in this position causes the fly to swim upside-down along the bottom, lessening the chance of it getting snagged up.

Hook	Long shank 10–12
Thread	Prewaxed brown or black
Tail	Brown partridge hackle fibers
Body	Olive antron or other fur
Rib	Fine oval gold tinsel
Hackle	Brown partridge or similar game bird feather
Thorax	Brown antron with a bead slipped onto a cut-down pin which is bent slightly with an upward tilt

Sedge Pupa

I was sent this pattern by Sigverdt (Steff) Steffensen of Tranbjerg, Denmark. The pattern is one of a series tied by Karsten Fredrikson, an innovative Danish fly-dresser with many realistic adult and pupal sedge patterns in his range.

Hook	Caddis-type hook, 8–12
Thread	Prewaxed brown
Underbody	Green lurex or similar colored tinsel
Overbody	Cream latex, stretched tight over the tinsel so that the color shows through
Wing	Gray duck
Thorax	Hare's fur
Antennae	Two strands of golden pheasant tail fibers curved over the back

Black Stone

I picked up this pattern in a fly shop in Missuola, Montana, where it is used on the Clarke Fork of the mighty Columbia River. It is fished weighted.

Hook	Long shank 6–12
Tail	Two black goose biots
Body	Black dubbed rabbit fur
Rib	Black nylon monofilament
Wing case	Dark turkey or similar feather fiber
Thorax and legs	Rabbit fur spun so that it flares out at the sides
Antennae	Two black goose biots

Pheasant and Orange

This fly was created by the well-known French author and fisherman Raymond Rocher. It works well as a possible caddis pupae. It is normally weighted with lead or copper wire and fished fairly deep.

Hook	All sizes
Thread	Prewaxed black or brown
Tail	Cock pheasant tail fibers
Body	Orange floss silk
Rib	Fine oval gold tinsel (optional)
Back	Cock pheasant tail fibers

Eel Skin Shrimp

This fly was devised by Ljubo Pintar of Most Na Soci, Slovenia and is one of the most unusual fly patterns I have ever received: the back of the fly is made from eel skin and the body from the tail of a dormouse. Ljubo Pintar is one of the most successful fly fishermen for big Marble trout (*Salmo mamoratus cuvier*) in the area of the River Soca. I also have examples of this shrimp tied for the River Gacka in Croatia, but down to size 16–18.

Hook	Curved sedge hook, 10–18
Thread	Prewaxed brown or olive
Tail	Short tuft of cock hackle fiber, either olive or gray
Body	Fur from a dormouse tail either undyed gray or dyed olive
Rib	Clear nylon
Back	Eel skin taken from the area where the back of the eel joins the belly

Annie's Nymph

This highly realistic fly was created by John Morton of Christchurch, New Zealand. The name Annie is derived from the scientific name for the dragonfly family Anisoptera. The body is woven from strips of olive and brown Swannundaze.

Hook	Long shank 10–12
Thread	Prewaxed black
Underbody	Dyed-green dubbed rabbit fur over a lead-formed body
Overbody	Woven Swannundaze olive and brown numbers 17 and 19
Wing case	Mottled turkey
Legs	Dyed-green partridge

Emerging Sedge

The creator of this and many other interesting nymphs and emerger patterns, is Andrija Urban who comes from Skopje in Macedonia. He mixes the body dubbing for most of his flies from antron and a range of natural furs such as rabbit, hare, dormouse, and otter. Many of his patterns also use the cul-de-canard feathers.

Hook	10–12
Thread	Prewaxed black
Tail	Short tuft of bright green antron
Body	Brown/olive fur mixture
Rib	Fine gold wire
Hackle	A few fibers of partridge tied beneath
Wing	Cul-de-canard tied in at the tail end and looped over the fly
Head	As body

Hatching Caddis Pupa

One of many caddis patterns devised by Luis Antunez of Madrid, it works equally well on rivers and still waters.

Hook	Sedge hook 8–10
Thread	Prewaxed black
Tail	Sparse cock pheasant tail fibers
Body	Cream wool or poly yarn
Rib	Brown silk
Hackle	Brown partridge
Wing case	Cock pheasant tail
Thorax	As body
Antennae	Cock pheasant tail

3D Glass Buzzer (Red)

There have been many attempts to tie more realistic representations of the chironomid pupa, the most important item in the diet of still-water trout. Earlier imitations were thought to be too bulky in profile but this pattern, and others like it, would appear to solve this problem. This buzzer pattern can be tied in a wide range of colors to match the indigenous species found on various waters, including black, olive, and orange.

Hook	Heavyweight grub hook sizes 10–16
Thread	Red
Body	Red thread tied thinly
Rib	Pearl Mylar tinsel
Thorax	Same as body but built up slightly
Cheeks	Red Mylar tinsel
Breathers	A short tuft of white poly yarn

The whole body and thorax is coated in quick drying epoxy resin

C.D.C. Buzzer

This fly was devised by Eilie Bertain of Belgium and is another of these slimmer profiled chironomid pupal imitations with the addition of a tuft of cul-de-canard at the head that helps the fly hang in the surface film like a natural pupa prior to hatching. The interesting thing about this pattern is the gap between the dressing and the head and cul-de-canard breathers.

Hook	Lightweight grub hook size 10–14
Thread	Black (other colored thread to match color varieties, claret, olive, etc.)
Tail	White feather fiber
Body	As tying thread, varnished
Cheeks	Orange Mylar or similar material
Head	Black
Breathers	Tuft of cul-de-canard

Czech Nymph (Amber and Orange)

This fly, originally from the Czech Republic, is used for both trout and grayling mainly on rivers and streams. It is tied in a variety of color combinations to imitate natural free-swimming caddis larvae of the Hydropsyche and Rhycophila species. It is usually fished quite heavily weighted to get down to the riverbed where the natural larvae are to be found. The introduction of a tungsten bead into the dressing gives one an extra heavy fly for deeper and faster-flowing rivers.

Hook	Heavyweight grub hook (leaded)
Thread	Black
Body	Amber followed by orange dubbing
Rib	Fine gold tinsel with clear monofilament over
Thorax	Hare's ear
Back	Latex or similar material

Spectral Worm

The chironomid larva or bloodworm leaves the sanctuary of its tunnel in the mud to absorb oxygen in the more oxygenated parts of the water. Trout as well as other fish species relish the bloodworm. This pattern is simplicity itself and seems to be very effective when fished on the drop; it is taken as it sinks slowly to the bottom without any noticeable retrieve.

Hook	Heavyweight grub hook 10–12
Thread	Red
Body	Twisted Flexi Floss or similar product with a central rainbow bead

Magic Circle Buzzer (Red)

Circle hooks were first used by commercial long-line fishermen in the U.S. for fish such as tuna, where a very acceptable hook-up rate of 80 percent was achieved. To date, trout fishermen have not shown a great interest in this new hook but those who have used them on nymph patterns believe that there is a 30 percent success rate. One of the reasons for this very average success rate may well be the fact that the angler must steel himself not to strike on the take. Striking, the natural reflex of most of us, will pull the fly straight out of the fish's mouth.

Hook	Circle hook 8–12
Thread	Red
Body	Red Flexi Floss, varnished
Thorax	As body, built up and varnished
Cheeks	Gold holographic tinsel

Tex's Little Devil

This "corixa" type fly was tied by my late father-in-law Harry "Tex" Ranger with much success on only its first outing. It works well for both trout and grayling due to the tungsten bead tied at the head, which is heavy enough to take the fly down to where the fish are lying. I have used this fly in the U.K. and Slovenia. I tied it on size 10 hooks where it also proved highly successful for Arctic grayling on the Kazan River in Canada.

Hook	Down-eyed heavyweight size 10–14
Thread	Black
Body	White tinsel braid or white floss
Rib	Fine oval silver tinsel
Back	Black-dyed cock pheasant tail
Paddles	The ends of the back feather divided either side of the fly and trimmed
Head	Tungsten bead

Polish Woven Nymph

Another import from eastern Europe, this has proved to be highly popular in the U.K. and in the U.S. Like the Czech Nymph on page 129, these are caddis larvae imitations and are equally successful for trout and grayling.

Hook	Heavyweight grub hook size 10–14, weighted
Thread	Black
Tail	Cock hackle fibers, short
Body	Woven floss: various light and dark color combinations, dark on the back, light underneath
Wing case	Cock pheasant tail fibers
Legs	Cock pheasant tail fibers, clipped short

Detached-body Damselfly

There are many damselfly imitations mainly because the damsel nymph is an important item in the diet of the still-water trout. This pattern has a detached extended body of marabou feather.

Hook	Down-eyed heavyweight size 10–12
Thread	Cream or olive
Tail and body	Plaited marabou feathers tied off leaving unplaited feather for the tail
Rib	Fine oval gold tinsel
Wing case	Cock pheasant tail
Thorax	Yellow fur dubbing
Legs (hackle)	Summer duck substitute fibers either side of the body
Eyes	Small black dumbbell (this provides the weight for the nymph)

lures

Despite recent development, lures are not a new innovation. It is very likely that this form of trailing fly has a lineage as long, if not longer, than the conventional patterns that imitate insect life.

The Inuit of Alaska have been using lures made of polar bear hair for many years. The modern streamer/bucktail lure can be traced to the doyen of the American dry fly, Theodore Gordon, who was alleged to have fished for pike with a large, feathered fly in the late 1880s. He published the dressing around 1903 and called his unruly, far-from-dry fly the Bumblepuppy.

Although large streamer-type flies (other than the normal salmon flies), such as the multihook Terrors, have been used by British anglers, it is to America that we must look for the origin of most modern patterns. The majority of British lures are used on still waters, while in the U.S., most of their large flies have been devised for use on rivers.

Lures are large flies tied to represent indigenous baitfish or small fry of the area being fished. Even infant trout and salmon have not escaped the attention of the fly-dresser, since they are often eaten by their larger siblings.

Some of the more vibrantly colored lures could not possibly represent any small river fish; their purpose is to attract. Trout will attack these gaudy flies from anger or curiosity, and if the lure is sufficiently fish-shaped, that will prompt the feeding response, even if the color is unnatural.

Let me qualify what is meant by streamer and bucktail. Streamers are lures tied with feathered wings, usually cock neck or saddle hackles, or even a feather and hair combination. Bucktails, on the other hand, use hair as the winging medium. The original flies used hair from various deer tails for the wing. Today, flies using goat, calf, squirrel, and even yak are called bucktails, with some patterns using man-made fibers.

All species of game fish are taken on streamers and bucktails: Brown trout, Rainbows, Dolly Varden, Cutthroat, migratory sea-trout, Steelhead, Atlantic and some Pacific salmon, pike, and a whole range of saltwater sport fish.

The large fly is not the exclusive province of America and Great Britain. There are also hundreds of unique lures from New Zealand and a number of them are given here. The lures of New Zealand have influenced fly design in both Australia and South Africa.

Muddler Minnow

This is a particular favorite of mine and was created by Don Gapen of Anoka, Minnesota. It can be used in many guises: as a small fish; a large nymph; on the surface as a caddis fly or stonefly; or as grasshoppers and crickets. There are many color variations of this lure: black, white, orange. A number of patterns dispense with the wing slips entirely and use a basic hair wing of squirrel tail or bucktail.

Hook	All sizes long shank 4–10
Thread	Black or brown
Tail	Oak turkey slip
Body	Gold tinsel
Rib	Oval gold tinsel (optional)
Hackle	Collar of unclipped deer hair
Wing	Gray squirrel with oak turkey slips either side
Head	Clipped deer hair

Whiskey Fly

A British bucktail lure devised by Albert Whillock and used originally on Hanningfield reservoir in Essex. The original fly utilized a proprietary brand of self-adhesive silver tape on the body. It is more usual now to use the dressing given here.

Hook	Long shank 6–10
Thread	Orange
Body	Flat gold tinsel
Rib	Fluorescent red floss
Hackle	Hot orange cock
Wing	Orange bucktail or calf tail

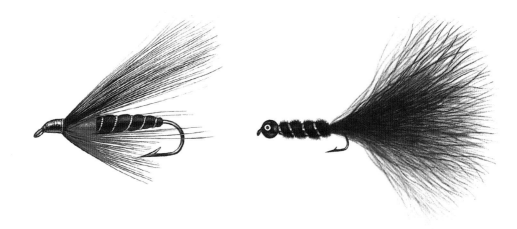

Sweeney Todd

This demon barber of a fly is perhaps one of the most famous by the late Richard Walker. A very killing "black lure" fly, the addition of the fluorescent throat enhances the pattern.

Hook	All sizes long shank 6–10; also tandem
Thread	Black
Body	Black floss, with fluorescent magenta wool at throat
Rib	Fine oval silver tinsel
Hackle	Crimson cock hackle fibers
Wing	Black squirrel

Dog Nobbler

One of the most recent killing lures on British reservoirs, it was devised by Trevor Housby, the well-known angling all-rounder. This fly has the rather dubious distinction of being one of the few flies to have its name registered. The fly itself is a development of American jigging lures. An almost identical fly, called Ice Fishing Fly, was tied by Bill Blades of the U.S. in 1951.

Hook	Long shank 6–10
Thread	Black
Tail	Black marabou (other colors: orange, white, pink, yellow, etc)
Body	Black chenille (or other colors to match tail)
Rib	Oval silver tinsel (optional)
Hackle	Sometimes a collar hackle is added to match body and tail color
Head	Lead shot painted with eye if desired

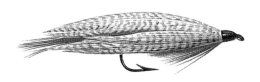

Appetizer

A fly devised by Bob Church, one of Britain's leading still-water anglers. This fly imitates the fry of such coarse fish as the roach. It can, on its day, be a very killing pattern indeed.

Hook	Long shank 6–10
Thread	Black
Tail	Mixed orange, green, and silver mallard fibers
Body	White chenille
Rib	Oval silver tinsel
Hackle	As tail
Wing	White marabou with gray squirrel over

Missionary

This pattern is a modern reservoir-lure version of a much older wet fly, the dressing of which was published in Courtney Williams's *Dictionary of Trout Flies*. He credits the invention of the original Missionary to Captain J. J. Dunn, and it was used on Blagdon Water in the U.K. Williams also gives an orange-hackled version. The original flies were developed by Dick Shrive, another Midlands reservoir stalwart, into the lure given here.

Hook	Long shank 6–10
Thread	Black
Tail	Red cock hackle fibers
Body	White chenille
Rib	Flat silver tinsel
Hackle	Red cock
Wing	Gray mallard breast feather tied flat on top of the hook

Black and Orange Marabou

The first time I used this fly, I caught two fish on successive casts. Both fish were about 3 lb in weight, which in those days was classed as very good fish, and on that day no other fly seemed to work. The Black and Orange Marabou has continued to catch fish wherever I have used it.

Hook	Long shank 8
Thread	Black
Tail	Orange cock hackle fibers
Body	Flat gold tinsel
Rib	Oval gold tinsel
Hackle	Hot orange cock
Wing	Black marabou with Jungle cock cheeks

Black Shimma

I based this fly on an American West Coast fly called the Black Bugger. I added some strands of a highly shimmering tinsel—which I have called Shimma—to the tail. The fly caught fish in vast numbers at the tail-end of the 1984 season, and continued to do so right through 1985 whenever the use of a lure was called for. The universally accepted name today is Crystal Hair. This lure can be tied in any color that takes your fancy.

Hook	Long shank 6–10
Thread	Black
Tail	Large tuft of black marabou with about eight strands of silver Shimma (this is a twisted metallic thread)
Body	Black chenille
Hackle	Palmered black cock

Orange Marabou Muddler

The original Muddler traveled westward and was adapted by Dan Bailey of Montana, U.S. He enhanced an already-effected pattern with a mobile marabou feather hackle. The white and orange version is depicted here; other flies in the series are black, white, yellow, brown, and green.

Hook	Long shank 4–8
Thread	Black
Tail	Red cock hackle fibers
Body	Gold tinsel chenille
Hackle	Unclipped deer hair
Wing	Orange marabou and three or four strands of peacock sword
Head	Clipped deer hair

Polystickle

This pattern devised by Richard Walker owes a lot to an earlier fly invented by Ken Sinfoil. He called his pattern Sinfoils Fry. In order to give the fly a transparent effect like the real fry it was imitating, Ken used a strip of polythene wound around for the body. Richard Walker adapted this polythene body by using raffene (Swiss straw). The best polythene to use is gauge 250. The raffene must be dampened before stretching it over the fly's back.

Hook	Long shank 8–10 (can be silvered or nickel hook)
Thread	Black or brown
Tail	Raffene (Swiss straw)
Body	Build a fish shape with a polythene strip; an underbody of red floss or wool can be added at the throat
Hackle	Cock to match the raffene
Back	Raffene

Jersey Herd

Another fry-imitating fly, this time created by Tom Ivens, one of the major influences on modern still-water fishing. The name Jersey Herd came from the fact that the tinsel on the original fly was cut from a Jersey milk bottle top. An equally effective body can be made from the yarn Goldfingering in a bronze color.

Hook	Long shank 8–10
Thread	Black
Tail	Peacock herl
Body	Flat copper tinsel over an underbody of silk
Hackle	Collar hackle of hot orange
Back	Bronze peacock herl
Head	Bronze peacock herl

Goldie Lure

A very good fly for murky water conditions; yellow is a very good color for such conditions and a contrasting yellow/black is even better. This is a favored pattern for Alan Pearson, holder of the British records for Rainbow and Brook trout.

Hook	Long shank 6–10
Thread	Black
Tail	Yellow hackle fibers
Body	Flat gold tinsel
Rib	Gold wire
Hackle	Yellow cock hackle fibers
Wing	Yellow goat with black goat over

Viva

A very popular fly on some waters, this is a simple black lure with a fluorescent green tail. The color fluorescent green is the most attractive to the trout. Alternative winging mediums for this pattern are black squirrel, black goat, or black marabou, and sometimes a combination of hair and marabou. An equally effective fly is the white version, the White Viva. The tail is the same in both patterns; just change white for black for the rest of the fly.

Hook	Long shank 6–10
Thread	Black
Tail	Fluorescent green wool
Body	Black chenille
Rib	Flat silver tinsel
Hackle	Black cock hackle fibers
Wing	Four black cock hackles (some prefer a wing of black squirrel)

Alaska Mary Ann

A classic American bucktail fly, this is based on a primitive Inuit ice-fishing lure called the Kobuk Hook, a jig used by the Inuit of the Kotzebue area of Alaska. Apparently, it was made with a sliver of whalebone or walrus ivory, a nail, and some polar bear hair. This particular fly was adapted by Frank Dufresne in the early 1950s.

Hook	Long shank 4–10
Thread	Black
Tail	Red cock hackle fibers (sometimes scarlet wool)
Body	White chenille
Rib	Silver tinsel
Wing	White calf tail (the original called for polar bear). Jungle cock cheeks (optional)

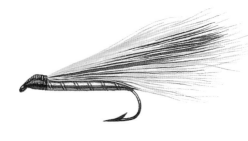

Spruce

One of the most popular West Coast streamer patterns for Cutthroat, Rainbow, and Brown trout. It was combined with a pattern called the Muddler to form the Spuddler.

Hook	Long shank 4–10
Thread	Black
Tail	Four or five peacock sword points
Body	One-third red floss silk; the rest thickly tied peacock herl
Hackle	Collar hackle of badger cock
Wing	Two badger hackles usually tied splayed out

Mickey Finn

Perhaps one of the best-known American streamer or bucktail patterns, this can be tied either as a hair-wing or as a feathered lure. The original name was Red and Yellow and was rechristened the Mickey Finn in the late 1930s. It has also been tied up as a salmon fly.

Hook	Long shank 6–10
Thread	Black
Body	Embossed silver tinsel (or flat silver tinsel)
Rib	If flat tinsel is used for the body then an oval silver rib is required
Wing	In three parts: yellow bucktail divided by a bunch of red bucktail

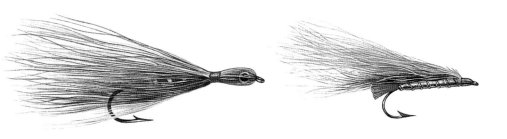

Thunder Creek Red Fin

This is one of a series of bucktail lures created by the American fly-dresser Keith Fulsher, a banker from Eastchester, New York. All of the Thunder Creek series are tied in the same way with the back and wing tied down to form the head of the fly. All the flies imitate a variety of small indigenous baitfish.

Hook	Long shank 8–10
Thread	Red
Body	Red floss
Rib	Flat silver tinsel
Back	Brown bucktail
Belly	White bucktail. Bound down to form the head
Head	Yellow eye, black pupil

Black-nosed Dace

This pattern was tied by one of America's leading fly-tiers and fishing authors Art Flick. It works very well on British still waters as a general fry imitation.

Hook	Long shank 6–10
Thread	Black
Tail	Short tuft of red wool
Body	Embossed silver tinsel (or flat silver tinsel)
Rib	None if embossed. If flat silver body, then oval silver tinsel is required
Wing	In three parts: brown bucktail, over black bear, over white bucktail

Black Ghost

An American streamer fly that has served many fishermen well in the U.K., myself included. On one occasion this fly won me a charity fly-fishing match against the Houses of Parliament team. The water that particular day was so murky that it needed a fly that the fish could see. The Black Ghost was the answer. The contrasting black body and white wing with yellow was highly visible to the fish. The fly originated in Maine.

Hook	Long shank 6–10
Thread	Black
Tail	Yellow hackle fibers
Body	Black floss
Rib	Flat silver tinsel
Hackle	Yellow cock hackle fibers
Wing	White cock hackles. Jungle cock cheeks (optional)

Gray Ghost

Perhaps one of the U.S.'s best-known streamer patterns, it was tied to imitate a smelt baitfish. The originator of this fly was Mrs. Carrie G. Stevens. The pattern dates from around 1924 and is one of a number of streamer lures credited to this fly-tier. All of Mrs. Stevens's flies were recognizable by a ring of red varnish or tying thread applied to the head of the fly.

Hook	Long shank 4–10
Thread	Black
Body	Orange floss
Rib	Flat silver tinsel
Hackle	A few strands of white bucktail, four strands of peacock sword, golden pheasant crest curving upwards
Wing	Four gray cock hackles over a bunch of white bucktail, flanked by silver pheasant body feather. Jungle cock cheeks (optional)

Yellow Matuka

The Matuka style of winging comes from New Zealand, where it was used on flies for the famous lakes Taupo and Rotorua. The Matuka is a bittern, now a protected bird so its feathers are no longer used in fly dressing. Hen pheasant flank makes a good substitute. Any fly which has the wing tied down by the ribbing tinsel is termed "Matuka"-style. This pattern is a useful fly in cloudy water conditions.

Hook	Standard size 4–10 or long shank 6–10
Thread	Black
Body	Yellow chenille
Rib	Oval silver or gold tinsel
Wing	Hen pheasant flank feathers tied down with the ribbing tinsel

Matuka Sculpin

This American fly is a development of the renowned Muddler Minnow. The addition of the Matuka-style wing gives us a more realistic imitation of the Sculpin minnow. In Great Britain the fly imitates the small fish called the Miller's Thumb or Bullhead.

Hook	Long shank 4–6
Thread	Amber
Tail	None (this is formed by the wing)
Body	Light amber sparkle yarn
Rib	Fine oval gold tinsel
Hackle	Unclipped deer hair
Wing	Speckled hen saddle hackle, or mottled partridge tail tied Matuka-style. Side fins are two mottled hen body feathers on either side
Head	Clipped deer hair. The deer hair can be left natural or marked along the top with a brown felt-tip pen

Red Split Partridge

A popular New Zealand fly, again tied Matuka-style but this time the wing is a mottled center tail from a gray partridge. The feather is split down the middle into two halves, placed back to back and tied on top of the hook with the oval tinsel rib. Alternative versions can be created by using different colors.

Hook	2–8
Thread	Black
Tail	Brown cock hackle fibers
Body	Red chenille
Rib	Oval silver tinsel
Hackle	Brown cock hackle fibers
Wing	Partridge tail

Red Setter

This New Zealand fly is used by many fly fishermen in South Africa. According to Hugh McDowell, one of New Zealand's leading fly tiers and a good friend of mine, this fly is the first choice of many beginners to fly fishing. The materials used in its construction are both inexpensive and readily available.

Hook	2–8
Thread	Black
Tail	Brown squirrel tail
Body	Orange chenille
Hackle	Two ginger cock hackles: one at the head and the other halfway down the shank

Parsons' Glory

A classic New Zealand pattern devised by Phil Parsons, one of the pioneers of Taupo fishing. The pattern is supposed to resemble a Fingerling trout.

Hook	2–10
Thread	Black or yellow
Tail	Red or orange cock fibers
Body	Yellow chenille
Rib	Oval silver tinsel
Hackle	Honey grizzle (light cree)
Wing	Honey grizzle cock hackles tied Matuka-style. Jungle cock cheeks (optional)

Mrs. Simpson

A famous New Zealand fly pattern presumably named after Wallis Simpson who became the Duchess of Windsor. The fly is used in the United Kingdom and also South Africa.

Hook	2–8
Thread	Black
Tail	Black squirrel tail
Body	Yellow or red wool or chenille
Wing	Tied along the sides of the fly, cock pheasant green rump

Yellow Rabbit

The first time I used a Rabbit fly, I was looking down onto a clear pool. I carelessly dropped my fly over the bridge to watch its action in the water. As I watched, two Rainbow trout gave chase along with a darting perch and finally a Jack pike. As with many of the New Zealand flies, a range of different colored bodies is possible.

Hook	2–8
Thread	Black or yellow
Tail	Cock hackle fibers, red or yellow
Body	Yellow chenille (other colors can be used)
Rib	Oval silver tinsel
Hackle	Yellow cock (other colors to match body color)
Wing	A strip of rabbit skin

Walker's Killer

The premier fly of South Africa. It appears that any South African fly fisherman who did not use this pattern would be considered a heretic. In recent years the fly has received a degree of popularity in the U.K., due mainly to the fact that a high proportion of the commercially dressed flies sold there are tied in South and East Africa.

Hook	Long shank 4–10 or normal shank 2–8
Thread	Black
Tail	Black squirrel
Body	Red chenille
Wing	Striped partridge hackle, tied along the sides in three sets of three hackles

Wiggle Sculpin

Two Sculpin imitations, the Muddler and the Matuka Sculpin, have already been mentioned. This fly from Roman Moser of Austria is even more realistic. It moves exactly like the small fish it is supposed to represent. Roman Moser's flies are strongly influenced by such American tiers as Dave Whitlock.

Hook	Lowater salmon size 6 linked during tying to a similar size hook with bend removed
Thread	Brown
Tail	Polypropylene fibers
Body	Extra thick chenille, marked after tying with a brown waterproof pen
Hackle	None, but two tufts of polypropylene as side gills
Head	Two yellow glass eyes

Whitlock's Sculpin

Perhaps one of the best-known and most sold sculpin patterns around, it is tied in the New Zealand Matuka-style and its head of clipped and shaped deer hair incorporates two and sometimes three stacked or banded deer hair colors.

Hook	Long shank 2–8
Thread	Olive or brown
Body	Light olive wool or yarn
Rib	Oval gold tinsel
Wing/tail	Four olive-dyed grizzle hackles tied down with the ribbing tinsel
Throat/gills	Red wool, yarn, or fur dubbing
Fins	Olive-dyed speckled hen feathers
Collar	Olive-dyed deer hair on top of the hook only
Head	Olive, black, and sometimes brown deer hair spun, muddler-style, and then clipped to shape

Trout and Salmon Parr Streamer

This is one in a series called Match the Minnow, devised by Dave Whitlock. It includes Black Nose Dace, Brook Smelt, Thread Fin Shad and Golden Shiner. All are tied upside down and in the same style as the pattern shown.

Hook	Long shank straight eye 4–8
Thread	White
Body	Mylar pearlescent tube secured at both ends
Underbody	Aluminum, lead or similar stiff foil cut to shape
Wing	Olive-dyed grizzle hackles either side of the bend of the hook and secured to the body with a coat of adhesive
Cheeks	Ringneck pheasant body feather
Head	Marked olive on top, white beneath
Eyes	Plastic doll's eye

Black Dahlberg Diver

This pattern was conceived by Larry Dahlberg and there are many variations— some with fur strip wings, others with flashabou tails, but most with marabou— all of which have one thing in common: the unique shape of the clipped deer-hair head. This pattern has a nylon weed guard.

Hook	Long shank straight eye 4–8
Thread	Red or black
Body	Wrapped silver braid
Wing	Black marabou, silver and pearl fine flashabou, with black cock hackles either side flaring outward. Topped with a few strands of peacock herl
Throat	A short tuft of red, silver, or pearl flashabou
Head	Black deer hair

Aschenhopper

Aschen is the German name for the grayling *Thymallus thymallus*, and this pattern was tied by Bavarian Werner Steinsdorfer. This fly is a cross between a nymph and a lure.

Hook	A special hook with a preformed lead shape. I believe these hooks are used in the construction of jigs for bass, etc. All sizes
Thread	Black
Tail	Tips of black ostrich herl
Body	Black ostrich
Rib	Oval silver tinsel
Wing	A few strands of gray speckled mallard flank
Head	Preformed lead shape, lacquered black
Eyes	White with red pupil

Aelvin

I devised this pattern some years ago based on the eel-skin flies used for sea-trout. It works well for both Brown and Rainbow trout and it is not too difficult to tie, even for beginners.

Hook	Long shank 8–12
Thread	Black or white
Tail	Pearl crystal hair in a short tuft
Body	PVC pearl sheet, marked with waterproof pen and folded over the hook
Underbody	Fluorescent red floss
Egg Sac	A bunch of orange Glo Bug yarn
Eyes	Plastic doll's eyes, glued on

Bow River Bugger

A cross between two effective flies, the Muddler Minnow and the infamous Woolly Bugger, the pattern is named after the famous Bow River in Alberta, the home of big Rainbows.

Hook	Long shank 2–8
Thread	Black
Tail	Black marabou with a few strands of blue flashabou
Body	Olive chenille
Hackle	Short palmered grizzle
Collar	Gray deer body hair
Head	Clipped gray deer hair with white deer in front, clipped muddler-style

The Mouse

Strictly speaking, I should have placed this fly in the dry-fly section, as this deer-hair concoction is dragged across the surface for large Alaskan Rainbow trout and other fish in that Mecca for all fly fishermen. This tied-up pattern also has a loop of nylon tied beneath the hook as a weed guard.

Hook	4–6 (the shank can be bent into a slight curve)
Thread	Prewaxed brown
Tail	A strip of leather
Body	Deer hair, clipped beneath and unclipped on top
Head	Clipped deer hair
Ears	Strips of leather cut to shape
Whiskers	Fine moose mane or similar hair
Eyes	Black varnish

Thread Fin Shad

This is one of the Janssen Fry series which imitate a range of small baitfish, created by American Hal Janssen. The body is made from silver Mylar slipped onto a preformed shape; it is then painted with acrylic paint and coated with epoxy resin. Four round black spots are painted on with an appropriate colored back and white belly. All the flies in this series are examples of the very finest in innovative fly-dressing. Larger flies tied in the same way are used for saltwater fly-fishing.

Hook	Long shank 4–8
Thread	Prewaxed grey
Tail	A tuft of short-fibered gray marabou
Body	Mylar tubing painted as described above then coated with epoxy resin
Eyes	White with black pupil

Soft Shell Crayfish

The trout and the black bass both relish a nice large crayfish. This American pattern is one of a color series: Orange, Green, and Sandy. All are dressed upside-down and in reverse. The pattern has also been used in all sizes for a wide variety of saltwater fish.

Hook	Long shank 2–8
Tail and back	Orange raffene (Swiss straw) marked with a waterproof pen
Body	Orange poly dubbing or antron
Rib	Fine monofilament
Legs	Grizzle hen dyed orange
Mouthparts	Short tuft of orange deer hair
Eyes	Black beads
Antennae	Moose mane or orange-dyed monofilament
Claws	Orange-dyed hen pheasant body feathers or similar game-bird feathers. These are lacquered

Midnight Rustler

This pattern was devised for night-time fishing on New Zealand lakes such as Rotarua and uses the feathers from the indigenous New Zealand bird, the Pukeko, an antipodean species of rail. The blue-black feathers are extremely mobile in the water. This particular fly, sent to me by Garth Coghill of Rotarua, uses two distinct tying styles: the usual side wing combined with a Matuka wing. The pattern represents a small baitfish called the Bully.

Hook	2–8 (a black-finished hook is an advantage)
Thread	Prewaxed black
Body	Black silk
Rib	Oval silver tinsel
Wing	Pukeko tied Matuka-style, then Pukeko tied on the sides
Cheeks	Jungle cock

Cat's Whisker

This fly pattern is the creation of the English fly-dresser David Train of Swindon, Wiltshire. This is an all-round reservoir lure for all seasons. Its name comes from the few white cat's whiskers incorporated in the wing. Most fly-tiers either leave this out or use something like a few fibers of bucktail. I have had some success with this fly tied with a black marabou wing and tail.

Hook	Long shank 6–10
Thread	Prewaxed black
Tail	White marabou
Body	Fluorescent yellow chenille
Rib	Oval silver tinsel
Wing	White marabou with a few white bucktail hairs; or as the original, white whiskers
Eyes	Silver bead chain

Booby Blobby

The "Booby" is so-called because of the two ultra-large foam or polystyrene balls on the head of the fly. This particular fly is usually fished on a sinking line, the buoyant eyes keeping the fly off the bottom. Trout will take this fly even when static but a slow retrieve activates the lure in a most enticing manner. This style of fly is popular on many of the English reservoirs and large waters in the Midlands.

Hook	Short shank down-eyed size 6 (this size gives the correct gape without the bulky dressing interfering with the hooking potential of the fly)
Thread	Black
Body	Black Cactus chenille
Wing	Six strands of orange Mirror Flash
Head	Two booby foam-rubber eyes
Eyes	Optional

Mini Minkie

An excellent fry-imitating lure with plenty of integral movement when retrieved, as it uses a mobile fur strip. Though the original called for mink fur, it can be just as effective using more mundane rabbit fur. By adding "Booby" eyes to the fly the equally effective Minkie Booby can be created, which can be excellent as a wake fly imitation. The Minkie has gained a worldwide reputation for taking big trout.

Hook	Short shank down-eyed heavy-weight sizes 6–10 (for larger flies use a long shank hook)
Thread	White
Tail and wing	Tan Mink Zonker strip
Body	White Light Brite with a Red Light Brite collar
Rib	Silver wire (this holds down the wing)
Head	Tying silk with optional eyes

Tandem Perch Fry

Towards the end of the season on large reservoirs throughout Britain, trout become preoccupied with feeding on the fry of many coarse fish such as roach, rudd, and perch. This particular pattern as its name suggests imitates the fry of the Striped perch. It uses a jointed hook assembly and can also be tied on a conventional long shank hook. The jointed version shown here gives a little more inbuilt wriggle to the lure. Other small fry can be tied in the same way.

Hook	Two ring-eyed hooks linked by fine strong wire (the hooks lie at the side and not underneath as is usual)
Thread	White
Tail	A short tuft of white marabou with olive marabou over
Body	White spun deer body hair, marked with waterproof pen
Eyes	Small epoxy eyes, glued in place

Golden Bullet Purple

Another lure that can be tied in a wide variety of colors—the purple is depicted here. This pattern is derived from the famous Woolly Bugger and has a distinct resemblance to Dave Whitlock's Lectric Leech, a fly used for American Large-mouthed bass.

Hook	Long shank 6–10
Thread	Purple
Tail	Purple marabou
Body	Purple chenille with a strip of gold holographic tinsel either side
Rib	Silver wire
Hackle	Purple-dyed cock
Head	Medium-size gold cone head

Golden Nugget Blob (Pearl)

This fly is more or less a sinking non-buoyant version of the Booby Blobby already depicted on page 153. Though garish to the eye it has accounted for many still-water specimen Rainbow trout. Like the Booby Blobby it can be tied in a wide variety of colors.

Hook	Short shank wide gape 6 (it can also be tied on a long shank hook)
Thread	White
Tail	Chartreuse Marabou
Body	Pearl Cactus chenille
Wing	Six strands of orange Mirror Flash
Head	¼ in. gold bead

Nomad

Another of these "sit up and look at me flies," a garish attractor that works well for Rainbow trout. Why the bright orange is effective in the capture of trout is an everlasting mystery, for there are few creatures swimming in the trout's environment so garishly colored.

Hook	Heavyweight down-eyed size 8–10 (can also be tied on larger long-shanked hooks)
Thread	Fluorescent orange
Tail	Hot orange marabou
Body	Orange Cactus chenille
Head	Gold bead with a tapered, varnished, fluorescent-orange thread nose

Polar Minnow

This fly originates in the U.S. where it is used as a successful lure for saltwater fly-fishing. It was used originally as a fly for Striper bass on the East Coast of America, but soon proved an excellent fly for many other saltwater species including tarpon. The Polar Minnow made the transition from the salt to freshwater where it became an excellent fly for imitating many small baitfish and fry.

Hook	Short shank straight-eye size 6 (can also be tied on long-shanked hooks)
Thread	White
Wing (includes body)	Built-up sections of Craft fur (sometimes called Polar Fur) marked with waterproof pens to match the color of the natural minnow. A few strands of silver tinsel are also added
Throat	Craft fur colored red
Eyes	¼ in. epoxy eyes

Leprechaun

There is a lake in the southeast of England that holds good-quality Brown and Rainbow trout and although I never caught any decent fish, everybody else did well. On one trip it reached the stage where I talked myself out of catching anything before I even started to fish, such was my lack of confidence. I mention this because the only fish I ever caught there was on a Leprechaun. This green lure was created by Peter Wood.

Hook	Long shank 6–10
Thread	Black or green
Tail	Green cock hackle fibers
Body	Fluorescent lime-green chenille
Rib	Flat silver tinsel
Hackle	Green cock hackle fibers
Wing	Four green cock hackles

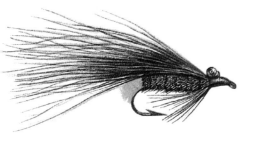

Rees's Lure

One of the best all-round lures, I have lost count of the number of fish it has caught around the world. I was first given the fly by Trevor Rees of Cardiff. Other versions are white, orange, and yellow.

Hook	Long shank 6–10; also on tandem linkage
Thread	Black
Tail	Fluorescent lime green
Body	Bronze peacock herl
Hackle	Black cock hackle fibers
Wing	Black marabou with black squirrel over
Eyes	Silver bead chain

Ace of Spades

A very killing fly created by Dave Collyer of Surrey, U.K. This fly is tied in the New Zealand Matuka-style with the wing bound down by the ribbing tinsel. This fly differs from the normal Matuka flies in that Collyer has overlaid the black main wing with a veiling of brown mallard. Why this makes a difference I do not know, but without this brown addition, the fly does not appear to be as killing.

Hook	6–12
Thread	Black
Body	Black chenille
Rib	Oval silver tinsel
Hackle	Guinea fowl hackle fibers
Wing	Tied Matuka-style with four black cock hackles, with bronze mallard over

Jack Frost

Another fly created by Bob Church, this white lure is at its best at the tail-end of the season when the big trout are chasing fry.

Hook	Long shank 6–10
Thread	White or black
Tail	Crimson wool
Body	White wool covered with a strip of wound polythene
Hackle	Crimson cock with white cock in front
Wing	White marabou

Badger Streamer

An attractive pattern devised by William F. Blades, a fly-dresser who was way ahead of his time. His book *Fishing, Flies and Fly-Tying* was published in 1951. The barred wood duck tail is a feature of many of Bill Blades's flies. The late Poul Jorgensen, a well-known American tier, was a student of Blades. Many so-called modern innovations can be found in the pages of Blades's book.

Hook	Long shank 6–10
Thread	Black
Tail	Barred wood duck flank
Body	Embossed silver tinsel
Hackle	Beard hackle of white bucktail
Wing	White bucktail, four badger hackles tied over, flanked by barred wood duck
Head	Black with white eye and black pupil

index

Acknowledgments

Executive Editor Trevor Davies
Project Editor Alice Bowden
Executive Art Editor Leigh Jones

Designer Ginny Zeal
Production Manager Ian Paton
Illustrators George Thompson and Kevin Jones